£4.95

a
d
Yacht
The legal aspects

Edmund Whelan
Barrister
and
Mandy Peters
F.Inst.L.Ex

Published by
The Royal Yachting Association
RYA House Ensign Way Hamble
Southampton SO31 4YA

Tel: 0845 345 0400
Fax: 0845 345 0329
Email: info@rya.org.uk
Web: www.rya.org.uk

CONTENTS _____

INTRODUCTION _____

The purchase of a yacht is probably one of the biggest investments the average owner will make in their life. Even a relatively modest cruiser capable of going offshore, is likely to cost tens of thousands of pounds, while a yacht large enough to cross an ocean in real comfort, with a few home luxuries aboard, will cost well over a hundred thousand.

And yet for all the expense and risk involved, the legal side of buying a yacht can be as simple as buying a box of matches.

The Merchant Shipping Act defines a 'ship' as 'every description of vessel used in navigation'. Thus any yacht is a ship, even down to the smallest sailing dinghy or powerboat. By the same token, any yacht owned by a British National is a British ship, entitled to registration on one of the British shipping registers, and also to all the rights and liabilities attaching to registered British ships under the Merchant Shipping Acts.

Unlike buying a house, it is possible for a yacht to pass through many hands, from one owner to another, without ever being registered, or without registration details being changed on each change of ownership. This is because a yacht is a chattel, rather than real property (like a house) and because registration is voluntary (unlike a motor vehicle where the Road Traffic Acts require every change of ownership to be notified to the Vehicle Licensing Authority).

The absence of formality does not in any way imply that the buyer of a yacht does not obtain good title. Although the first owner buying a new yacht will probably receive a Builder's Certificate and a receipted invoice from the builder or dealer, in many cases these documents are mislaid and subsequent buyers will often (unwisely) take over the yacht by a simple verbal agreement and no documentation.

Although a yacht can be bought and sold without formality and used without being registered, this is definitely not recommended. The purchase and use of a yacht is full of potentially expensive pitfalls for the uninitiated and experienced alike; the purpose of this book is to identify those pitfalls and guide the buyer on how to protect his investment and his peace of mind.

THE CONTRACT

It is a common fallacy among non-lawyers that a contract needs to be in writing to be binding on either party to an agreement. In fact this is not the case except for the sale of 'real property' (i.e. land, or a house) where the Law of Property Act specifically requires contracts to be in writing. A simple conversation on the following lines:

A. "I like the look of your yacht, how much would you sell her for?"

B. "She's yours for twenty thousand pounds"

A. "All right, I'll buy her for twenty thousand pounds,"

is sufficient to create a binding contract or agreement (the words are interchangeable).

So far as the seller is concerned, the simpler the deal the better. His only interest is to receive the money as soon as possible and shed his responsibilities for the care and upkeep of the yacht.

For the buyer however, the results of a quick verbal agreement of that sort could be absolutely disastrous. Unless he can be sure that the yacht and all the fittings are in good condition, that all VAT and taxes due on the yacht have been paid, that there are no yard, marina or salvage bills outstanding, that all the equipment to be sold with the yacht has been listed and agreed, that there are no outstanding mortgages or legal charges on the yacht, that all co-owners agree to the sale, that the actual ownership of the yacht will not pass to him before he has arranged full insurance cover and that the yacht is Recreational Craft Directive compliant or exempt (see chapter 6), he could be making a very expensive mistake.

However, a methodical approach to buying the yacht, leaving out any potentially expensive shortcuts, should ensure that most of these risks are minimised; the size of the investment obviously justifies a thoroughly cautious and even suspicious approach, unless both yacht and seller are well known to the buyer. The normal order of events is as described in Appendix 10.

Buying through a broker

Even if you are buying a yacht through a yachtbroker as opposed to a private buyer, the principal of 'buyer beware' still applies. The broker will be acting on behalf of his client, i.e. the seller, and not you, the buyer. Anyone can rent office space and start trading as a

yachtbroker. It is in the buyer's interest to dreams is a member
of the YBDSA, and, more importantly has Public Liability
Insurance. In the case of the latter you may sue him in the event
of failure to deliver the yacht, disclose a marine mortgage, or return
your deposit. In a case of doubt about the broker's credentials a
buyer may wish to appoint their own broker or solicitor to act on his
behalf during the purchase. The YBDSA will point you in the direction
of a reputable broker in your area. Alternatively the RYA can advise
on the choice of a specialist solicitor.

Buying direct

For buyers not buying through a broker or a solicitor, the starting
point will be one of the standard form contracts available either from
the broker (if one is involved in selling the yacht), or from the Royal
Yachting Association (reproduced in Appendix 1).

Bearing in mind the risk of entering into a binding agreement by a
verbal offer and acceptance, the careful buyer will ensure that no
commitment is made on his part until he has satisfied himself on
every aspect of the purchase.

Having found the yacht of his choice, and before negotiating the
price, he should make it clear to the seller that, if an offer is made,
it will be subject to a written contract being entered into. Where
the buyer intends to enter into a face to face bargaining session, it
would be advisable to have two copies of the standard form
contract ready to hand, so that the session can finish with both
parties signing the contract and being bound by its terms.

Once the price has been settled, the precise terms of the inventory
agreed, and all other points fully understood by both parties, the
relevant parts of the written contract should be completed, and the
documents signed, with each party taking a copy for his own use.

The standard form contract is reprinted in full at Appendix 1; it is
important that both parties understand fully the matters that are dealt
with in the contract, and the way in which the transaction proceeds
under the terms of the contract. The contractual terms are laid out in
the following sequence.

Parties

It may seem an obvious point, but both the vendor and the
purchaser need to be sure exactly who is buying and who is selling
the yacht. It is important that any joint owner of the vendor is
disclosed, and if the yacht is to be bought in the name of another

person (or company) this should be written into the contract. Also, if the yacht is registered in the name of a company (even a single shareholder company) it is essential that the sale is dealt with as a sale by the company, not the individual shareholder on a personal basis.

Purchase price and deposit

The conventional deposit is 10% of the agreed purchase price but there is no reason why the purchaser should not offer a lesser sum and amend the contract accordingly.

In fact there is a good argument for limiting the deposit to an amount sufficient to cover the cost of hauling out and relaunching the yacht for a survey, replacing any antifouling, fittings and furnishings disturbed by the purchaser's surveyor, and any other relevant costs.

Experience has shown that in some cases the vendor or his agent has been reluctant to repay the deposit where the purchaser wishes to reject the yacht after the surveyor has found material defects. The vendor may claim that the alleged material defects are too trivial to allow the purchaser to withdraw and refuse to refund the deposit, giving the purchaser no option but to resort to lengthy and expensive legal proceedings.

The purchase price, once agreed, is of course binding on both parties unless the purchaser is able to rely on Clause 5 of the contract (defects disclosed by survey) to offer a lower sum. In that case it is for the vendor to decide whether to accept or reject the lower offer.

Agreement for sale

The vendor's agreement to sell carries the legal implication that he has the right to sell, and that the yacht is free of any encumbrances, charges, liens etc. This is referred to in more detail in Clause 7.3 and is also enforceable under Section 12 of the Sale of Goods Act 1979. Advice on checking the vendor's title is given in Chapter 4.

The yacht and equipment

It may be that the vendor wishes to retain the name for his next yacht. If the yacht is on the Part 1 Register (see Chapter 3) the requirement for a unique name means that the purchaser will have to contract to change the name of the yacht after completion.

It is important for the purchaser to make an inventory of the machinery, equipment and gear as early as possible in the proceedings, as loose items worth many hundreds, even thousands of pounds, have a habit of walking once a price has been agreed. The inventory forms part of the contract and should be initialled by both parties after a joint inspection.

Value Added Tax and other dues

Many thousands of yachts are lying in overseas marinas and harbours, being used regularly by their owners, but without local VAT or other dues having been paid. Some overseas authorities are content with the situation until the yacht is sold, when the claim for VAT and dues might be backed up with the impounding of the yacht. Further advice is given in Chapter 5.

Inspection/survey

A survey is considered essential by most owners, and the contract is designed to provide a period between signing of the contract and completion for the survey to take place. Typically the purchaser will ask for 21 days to arrange a survey, but where both parties are keen to complete the transaction quickly, a surveyor can be instructed at a few days notice and requested to prepare a written report immediately after the survey. This need only take 2 or 3 days, depending on the availability of an experienced and qualified professional. Further advice on surveys is given in Chapter 2. It should be noted that all expenses involved in a survey, including yard fees and preparing the yacht for survey, are met by the purchaser.

Notice of defects/acceptance of yacht

The survey will normally disclose material defects that had not previously been seen on the purchaser's inspection. This will give the purchaser the opportunity to reject the yacht, cancel the contract and claim his deposit back, or propose to the vendor a lower price or the opportunity for the vendor to remedy the defects. The vendor of course has the right to reject a lower offer or a notice to remedy the defects and to look for an alternative purchaser. The contract provides a strict time framework for both the purchaser and the vendor to take action after the survey, and both should bear these time limits in mind at all times.

Completion of sale

The purchaser is required to pay the balance of the agreed price within seven days of the acceptance of the yacht.

If the yacht is on the Part 1 Register (see Chapter 3) the vendor should hand over the ship's papers at this time. In addition to the Certificate of Registry and Bill of Sale these should include the Builder's Certificate, the original VAT invoice, all contracts and Bills of Sale tracing ownership of the yacht from new to the present transaction, confirmation of RCD compliance or exemption, and all equipment manuals and service records. In practice many vendors are unable to produce much in the way of paperwork, but a valid Certificate of Registry, Bill of Sale, and proof of VAT payment or exemption (see Chapter 5) and RCD information should be regarded as essential. If the yacht is unregistered or on the Small Ships Register (see Chapter 3) proof of VAT payment or exemption, a simple Bill of Sale (Appendix 5), a Certificate of Registry and RCD information together with any other available documentation is essential.

Vendor's right to assign title

See under *Agreement for Sale* above. However, even though the vendor guarantees under this section that he has the right to sell, and that the yacht is free from any charge, the checks outlined in Chapter 4 should still be carried out.

Free access after completion

A yacht laid up ashore may have easy access at the time of the purchaser's initial inspection, but by the time completion has taken place the yacht may be blocked in by numerous other craft being laid up. Removal of the yacht by the purchaser's contractors can mean great additional expense as yachts are shuffled around the yard to make space for the removal.

Warranties

This section underlines the importance of a survey in buying a yacht from a private individual. **The Sale of Goods Act provisions about reasonable quality and fitness for purpose do not apply to private sales** and the vendor is under no duty to draw defects to the attention of the purchaser. If the vendor has made specific representations, statements, or promises about the yacht, that is a different matter, but proving such statements in court on a misrepresentation case is likely to be very much more costly and time consuming than commissioning a professional survey.

Risk

It is important that the risk in the yacht should not pass to the purchaser until he has completed his insurance arrangements (see Chapter 7).

Default

The contract provides for the rights of each party in the event of a default by the other. One point which over-optimistic purchasers often fail to realise until it is too late is that there is no provision in the contract for changes of mind. Once the contract is signed, and unless the survey discloses previously unseen material defects, the purchaser is bound to proceed with the transaction or risk losing his deposit and any additional costs (including the shortfall in price offered by a later purchaser) involved in a re-sale.

Arbitration

If a dispute does arise, it is preferable for the parties to agree to an informal arbitration before instructing solicitors. Legal proceedings should only be entered into after all other avenues of conciliation have been explored.

Entire agreement clause

The final clause in the contract provides that no other written or verbal statements should be taken into account by either party in interpreting the contract. This does not prevent the purchaser from taking legal action in respect of any misrepresentation by the vendor by which he was persuaded to enter into the contract. A representation does not form part of the contract and is not affected by this clause.

THE SURVEY

Provision is made in Clause 4 of the contract for the purchaser to have the yacht surveyed. Although the yacht may appear to be in excellent condition, and a survey may appear unnecessary, it is a sensible precaution to take. A surveyor will usually find sufficient hidden problems with the yacht to enable the buyer to reduce his first offer by at least the equivalent of the surveyor's fees; in more serious cases he can detect signs of potentially disastrous defects, and in any event his report will provide some level of guarantee since he will be legally liable for the costs of remedying any defects that he has negligently missed.

The detailed instructions given to the surveyor are of importance. It may simply be that a hull condition survey is required, or a full survey to include rig, sails, engine and all other equipment aboard. If the engine or engines form a substantial part of the value of the boat, it will probably be worthwhile having a separate detailed engineers report, which may include a sea trial and full report on the yacht's performance.

The surveyor should also be given a copy of the particulars of sale and asked to verify any technical aspects, or references to measurements or to the age of the yacht, that are important to the buyer. Even if apparently precise details have been included in a broker's information sheet, most such sheets contain a declaration that the particulars do not form part of any contract, and that buyers should check the accuracy of any statements for themselves.

Once the survey and engineers report (if any) have been received, the contract allows the buyer up to 14 days to decide on his next step. If the survey discloses no material defects, then the buyer is obliged to go ahead with the agreement. If on the other hand material defects are found which were not readily apparent on the buyer's initial inspection of the yacht, he has the option either of withdrawing from the sale and having his deposit refunded, renegotiating the price to allow for repairs or renewals, or requesting the seller to rectify matters at his own expense prior to completion of the contract.

Whether a defect is material or not is a frequent source of dispute between the parties. Although there is no exact definition as to what is material, it could be said that if the cost of remedying the defect or defects is more than 5% of the agreed value of the yacht then that is

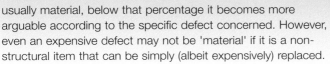

usually material, below that percentage it becomes more arguable according to the specific defect concerned. However, even an expensive defect may not be 'material' if it is a non-structural item that can be simply (albeit expensively) replaced.

When selecting a surveyor or engineer it is advisable to establish whether they have full professional indemnity insurance. The likelihood of a surveyor failing to detect a serious fault may be limited, but mistakes can be made and unless the surveyor carries insurance the buyer may find himself without financial redress. Most surveyors are members of a professional body such as the Royal Institution of Naval Architects or the Institute of Marine Engineers. There are however many who hold no formal qualifications but whose experience more than makes up for this. Membership of the Yacht Brokers, Designers and Surveyors Association is limited to those with relevant qualifications or experience, and indeed the YBDSA insists on all its surveying members carrying full professional indemnity insurance.

In bygone days the majority of yachts were built under Lloyds supervision, and this body still enjoys a worldwide reputation. However, in recent years a number of cases have arisen where the buyer of a yacht with a Lloyds certificate has found to his cost that it does not provide a full guarantee and financial indemnity against defects. There is no substitute for the buyer instructing his own surveyor and having a report prepared for his own purposes. A report prepared for another person (e.g. a prospective purchaser who has dropped out) may appear to cover all the buyer's points of concern, but it is unlikely that the buyer could take legal action against a negligent surveyor since the report was not prepared for him, or on his own instructions. However in some cases the surveyor may agree (for a fee) to be legally bound in respect of the previously prepared report.

REGISTRATION _____

As we have seen, registration for any size of pleasure craft within the United Kingdom is entirely voluntary. An owner may wish to register his craft for a number of different reasons, his reasons will dictate the form of registration he chooses.

Part 1 Registration

The Merchant Shipping Act 1995 provides for the registration of British-owned ships. Registration under Part 1 which is managed in Cardiff by the Registrar General of Shipping and Seamen, requires full details and proof of ownership to be provided by the applicant, together with a measurement survey report prepared by a qualified tonnage measurer. With measurement fee, certification fee, and the required marking of the vessel with the registered number, the total cost of registration is, at 2004 prices, £500, plus a five-yearly renewal fee of £50. However, since registration under Part 1 provides the owner with unquestionable evidence of title, it can make the later sale of the yacht very much simpler, as a purchaser need only satisfy himself that the seller is the registered owner, and the yacht is not subject to a registered mortgage.

Part III Registration (Small Ships Register)

The SSR was instituted in 1983 in response to the requirement of a number of overseas authorities for British owned yachts to be properly registered, and the reluctance of many yacht owners to pay the full registration fee required. The SSR provides a yacht owner going foreign with a Government issued document stating the name of the declared owner. The certificate is issued simply upon the completion of a form by the applicant and is of no value as proof, or even evidence, of ownership. However, since the cost is £12 for a 5 year certificate and entitles the registered owner to wear a privileged ensign (provided he is a member of a relevant club) and to carry duty free stores (if taking his yacht beyond the shores of the European Union), there are a great number of yacht owners who opt for Small Ships Registration in preference to Part 1 Registration.

Checking the register

For the prospective purchaser, checking the registers is the first and most obvious step that should be taken.

For a yacht on the Part 1 Register, the name and Port of Choice (or initials of the owner's club) should be marked on the stern, and the official number either carved in the main beam (at the deckhead adjacent to the main mast) of a wooden yacht, or displayed on a plaque on the main bulkhead in the case of a grp or metal-hulled yacht. The owner should also be able to show a certificate naming him as the registered owner. Having satisfied himself that the yacht is the one referred to (including a check on the engine serial number) the buyer should then contact the Registrar General of Shipping and Seamen in Cardiff and request a transcript of the registration particulars. This transcript should duplicate the information on the registration certificate, and in addition will also disclose whether any mortgage has been placed on the vessel. The buyer should beware however, since the Register does not allow for the reservation of title and, in theory, it is possible for an unscrupulous seller to enter into a mortgage agreement with a finance house (or even sell the yacht to another buyer) between the buyer's inspection of the register and completion of the sale, particularly if there is a delay between the two. As a matter of practice however, the Registrar General's office, having provided a written transcript to an enquirer, will provide further information free of charge over the telephone to the enquirer up to a week after providing the transcript. The address and telephone number of the Registry of Shipping and Seamen is given at Appendix 6.

For yachts on the Small Ships Register there is still some benefit in checking the registration particulars, as the limited information on the transcript may go towards building up a complete picture of the information provided by the seller.

Transfer of title

Once the buyer has completed his investigations of title and acted upon the results of the survey he will usually wish to go ahead with completion of the sale. Whether this is through a broker or privately he should not hand over the final balance of the purchase price unless he is given the relevant documentation to enable him to re-register the yacht in his own name. In the case of a Part 1 registered yacht, this will consist of the yacht's registration certificate in the seller's name, and a Bill of Sale made out in the name of the buyer and signed by the registered owner. If either of these is defective it will not be possible for the buyer to re-register the yacht in his own name, and he will often be put to great trouble and expense in remedying the problem. If the seller is unable at the last minute to produce exactly the right documentation, then the buyer should consider retaining a part of the price (perhaps 5% or 10% of the total) against receipt of the required documentation.

It often happens for example that a seller did not take the trouble to re-register the yacht in his own name when he originally acquired it. This does not signify that his beneficial ownership of the yacht is in doubt, but it would involve the new buyer having to trace the original registered owner to persuade him to sign the Bill of Sale in his favour. If this proves impossible (as is often the case) the buyer will have either to wait until the current registration lapses before re-registering the yacht in his own name, or make a formal application to the High Court for an order requiring the Registrar to transfer the title. These problems can be reduced by simple precautions at the time of completion.

Once the buyer has the Certificate of Registry and a Bill of Sale in his possession, these should be sent to the Registrar with the appropriate fee for change of particulars (£80 in 2004). An amended certificate will be sent back to the new owner in due course.

For yachts on the Small Ships Register the procedure is very much simpler. Since the Register entry and certificate are not evidence of title, the only check that can be carried out is an inspection of the Certificate for any sight of obvious fraud and an enquiry to the SSR Office. Upon completion of the purchase of a yacht on the Small Ships Register, the register lapses and a purchaser must re-register.

The cautious buyer will also carry out further checks as referred to in Chapter 4.

On completion of the sale the buyer is advised to obtain the signed contract, the original VAT receipt or exemption certificate, a receipt for the money paid, a completed Bill of Sale which will help if kept with the ship's papers and produced as evidence of title when he comes to sell the yacht on in due course, and the RCD confirmation.

CHECKING THE VENDOR'S TITLE

As we have seen, there is no legal requirement for a yacht owner to record his ownership on either of the official registers. This obviously has implications for a buyer when purchasing a yacht from a stranger, since in many cases he will not be sure that the seller has a bona fide right to sell, or that the yacht does not have a loan outstanding against it, which could (and all too often does) lead to it being repossessed by the finance company from the new owner.

Part 1 Registered Yachts

For yachts that are entered on the Part 1 Register, the position is relatively simple. A buyer can satisfy himself that the yacht is indeed the property of the alleged owner, and that there are no registered mortgages entered on the register, simply by contacting the Registrar General of Shipping and Seamen in Cardiff and asking for a transcript of the Register entry for that yacht. This is obtainable by post at a cost of £12 and the transcript will show who the registered owner is, and for how long he has been the registered owner, as well as any registered mortgages (name of lender only, not the amount of the original mortgage nor the amount outstanding).

Liens

The buyer should however remember that although the entry on the Part 1 Register indicates good title, and any unregistered mortgages are invalid against a bona fide purchaser without notice of them, it is still possible for other parties to have a lien or interest in the yacht. Harbour Authorities, marinas, boat repair yards, crew, salvors (if the yacht has been the subject of a salvage claim) victuallers, suppliers of equipment, or others, may all have a claim against the owner of a yacht, in which case they may also be able to claim a lien against the yacht itself, even when it has changed hands. This also extends to the VAT collection authorities if the yacht is VAT unpaid (or if the owner cannot prove that there is no VAT liability). It is of course impossible for an intending buyer to be completely satisfied that there are no liens outstanding on the yacht; the best he can do is ensure that the contract is signed (Clause 7.3 deals with liens, mortgages etc) and ask at the marina office, or the Harbour Master's Office if there are any known problems with the yacht. Word of any unpaid bills, marina charges, harbour dues or salvage claims tends to circulate very fast, and the local grapevine is probably the best means of accessing this information.

Yachts on the Part III (Small Ships) Register or unregistered

The SSR was originally set up by the Department of Transport under the Merchant Shipping Act 1983 for the simple purpose of providing an inexpensive alternative to Part 1 Registration for yachts going foreign. As we have seen (Chapter 3) registration of a yacht on the SSR is a simple matter of the owner filling in an application form and forwarding it to the Registry of Shipping and Seamen. The Register is not intended to be a title register, or even to be evidence of ownership, and a registration certificate carries a warning to this effect.

For yachts registered on the SSR, or yachts that are unregistered, there is no simple means by which a prospective purchaser can check the seller's title, or check that there is no financial charge on the yacht. Therefore, unless the seller and the yacht are known to the buyer, it makes sense to investigate the title, even if the sale is through a reputable broker, since he is under no duty to run any checks on the seller's bona fides.

Ideally the seller should be able to produce documents of title showing the chain of ownership from the time the yacht was built, down to the present time. These should include the original Builder's Certificate, the original receipted VAT invoice from the builder, and subsequent signed forms of contract and Bills of Sale from the first owner to the second, and so on until the present owner. The seller may also be able to provide evidence of recent mooring charges, harbour dues, insurance premiums, maintenance and repair work or racing certificates; if these are consistent with what is known about the seller and the yacht, and go back three or more years, then it is reasonable to assume that the yacht is his to sell. Even if the seller is entirely lacking in any documentary evidence of his ownership, (and this is not unusual), he should still be able to refer the buyer to a yacht club officer, a Harbour Master, a river or canal authority, or a boatyard. Except in the case of the very smallest boats moved from place to place on a trailer, any seller who is unable to refer a buyer to someone reliable in authority or in the boating business should be treated with caution.

Checking on the absence of an unregistered mortgage is a rather more difficult matter. In the High Court case of *The Shizelle* (1992), it was held that an unregistered mortgage on an unregistered yacht was valid not only against the original borrower, but also against any subsequent owner whether or not he knew of the mortgage. Given that a number of leading finance houses lend considerable sums of money on the basis of unregistered mortgages, this creates an obvious danger for buyers. In recent years a number of cases have occurred where a buyer in good faith has had his boat repossessed by the defaulting seller's finance house. In some cases this does not occur until months or years after the sale, and is usually triggered off by the seller missing one or more of his repayment installments.

In the absence of any official documentation whatsoever the buyer needs at least to satisfy himself that the owner is who he says he is, lives where he says he does, and that the yacht in question is the same vessel described in the Sales Agreement. You may have to make enquiries as to where the boat has been kept, ask yards if they have ever done any work on her, and ascertain whether or not she owes any yards any money. If the owner belongs to a sailing club then that is a good place to start. It is also advisable to check with all the major marine finance houses (listed in Appendix 4) to confirm whether or not they have an interest in the yacht in question. If you have employed another broker or solicitor yourself then you can safely leave this to him, and as a professional he will probably elicit more direct responses than you will as an unknown or lay person.

When all of the above has failed or is unavailable, a five year period must elapse before eligibility for Part 1 Registration is automatically assumed. Although SSR registration can be effected immediately you will be unable to re-register her your own name on Part 1. This may depress the value of the boat considerably since many buyers would be reluctant to take on a yacht with no proof of title (which of course the SSR does not provide).

Boatmark scheme

In 1995, in response to numerous cases of finance fraud, and also to discourage the theft of yachts and yacht equipment, the British Marine Federation set up the Boatmark scheme in collaboration with HPI Equifax. Once fully established, it is hoped that all finance agreements on yachts in the UK will be recorded and information made readily available to potential purchasers. The Boatmark scheme is based on the Hull Identification Number introduced by the British Marine Federation in the mid 80s to provide every boat in the country with a unique identifying code number. Each boat has its number clearly marked on the upper starboard corner of the transom, either during construction or at one of over a hundred marking stations around the country. This number becomes the key identifier for the record of that particular craft which Boatmark maintains in a database linked with the Police National Computer.

The boat's keeper receives a Certificate showing details of the craft, the date of first registration, and the name and address of the keeper. When the boat is sold prospective purchasers are able to confirm the validity of the information on the Certificate by a simple phone enquiry and vendors have a ready means of demonstrating their craft's background.

At the time of writing (2004) the scheme has yet to attract wide support from the finance houses, yacht brokers, insurance indemnifiers or private boat owners themselves.

Unless and until the scheme becomes fully established, potential purchasers of SSR or unregistered yachts will still be advised to carry out the checks outlined above.

Documentation

It is important when checking documentation to have sight of original copies, and not to rely on photocopies which can easily be falsified.

VAT LIABILITIES

Value Added Tax was introduced in the United Kingdom in 1972, as a tax on the supply of services, and on the sale or import of goods. Any yachts built in or imported into this country for private use since that date should be VAT-paid and ideally a seller of a yacht should be in a position to provide the buyer with the yacht's original VAT receipt, or at least a copy certified by the builder or original supplier as being a true copy. Unless the seller is able to produce proof that VAT on the yacht has been paid at some time, either in the United Kingdom or elsewhere in the EU, the buyer should be ready to face a potential VAT assessment on the current value of the yacht at any time an EU Customs official carries out a spot check.

Until the end of 1992 it was possible for a yacht built in the UK, for a UK resident, to be exported immediately upon completion without payment of VAT, for use overseas on a tax-free basis. The International Convention on Temporary Importation provided that all convention countries should permit the free use of recreational equipment and 'means of transport' for touristic purposes for a minimum of six months in any one year. This rule was interpreted more liberally than the minimum in most European countries including France, Spain and Italy, and over the years tens of thousands of yachts built for northern European owners enjoyed tax free status in Mediterranean marinas.

The completion of the Single Financial Market on 1st January 1993 saw the end of concessions of this sort between EU States. Apart from a few months' grace for yachts already enjoying tax-free status, any yacht in any EU State, owned by a national of any EU State for his private use, must be VAT-paid. In theory it should make little difference which State the VAT is paid in, since rates are intended to be roughly equivalent (see Appendix 7 for details of 2004 rates). In practice however, experience has shown that some States tend to be considerably more flexible in agreeing modest valuations with owners, and allowing payments to be spread over an extended period. At the time of writing, the Customs and Excise authorities in the UK are apparently not prepared to discuss valuations or payment terms unless a yacht is actually within the UK (by which time it is obviously too late to negotiate). The importer of a yacht from outside the EU will therefore find it to his advantage to import it first to another EU State where a valuation and payment terms have been agreed in advance (in writing) before bringing it into this country. Once a yacht has been imported into any EU State and VAT paid, in theory no further VAT liability can arise within the EU.

The completion of the Single Financial Market on 1st January 1993 also saw the introduction of an amnesty for any yacht in the EU area built on or before 31st December 1984. Therefore unless a yacht owner in the EU is able to prove

either that the yacht is VAT paid
or that it was built before 31st December 1984
and was in EU waters on 31/12/92 - 1/1/93,

he is liable to pay VAT on the current value of the yacht, and there are likely to be spot checks in any EU State on any yacht at any time.

The potential VAT liability is something that all intending purchasers must be aware of. If the seller of the yacht cannot produce full documentary evidence of non-VAT liability, then arguably the yacht is worth only 100/117½ of the asking price.

In 1998 HM Customs and Excise published an information sheet reprinted in Appendix 8.

RECREATIONAL CRAFT DIRECTIVE

Most people will be aware that importing a yacht from overseas will involve payment of VAT and Import Duties; but many forget the requirement for the yacht to comply with the Recreational Craft Directive. Lack of awareness of this requirement can prove to be extremely costly.

The purpose behind the RCD is to allow a single European market in recreational craft to operate.

Since 16th June 1998, all recreational craft with few exceptions, between 2.5 and 24 metres in length, sold or put into service in the European Economic Area (EEA) for the first time must comply with the essential safety requirements of the RCD, and must be CE marked to certify compliance. This includes imported yachts either new or secondhand, and home built yachts if placed on the market within five years of completion, which are intended for sports and leisure purposes. The builder, his agent, or the person importing the boat is responsible for compliance and marking.

The EEA includes all EU countries plus Iceland and Norway. A list of EEA countries can be obtained from the Technical Unit of the RYA.

A yacht that comes within the scope of the RCD must have accompanying documentation. These include a Technical File, and an Owner's Manual which must include a written Declaration of Conformity. The yacht should also carry a CE compliance plaque in a prominent place.

The Amending Directive

The Amending Directive; is intended to allow a single European Market in recreational craft to operate whilst maintaining a high level of environmental protection.

The Amending Directive has been agreed (2004), and is set to apply to a wide variety of new recreational craft, including sail cruisers over a certain size, motor cruisers, motor boats and personal watercraft, whether powered by outboard, stern drive, or inboard engines. The changes will also apply to existing craft and their engines that undergo major modification and conversions.

It introduces a further set of essential safety requirements, which include requirements as to emissions.

EU Member States must comply with most of its measures from 1st January 2005. However, there is a further transitional period of 1st January 2007 in relation to compression, four-stroke ignition engines and two-stroke ignition engines.

Both Directives are enforced by Trading Standards Departments of Local Authorities. Breach of either of the Directives may result in a fine of up to a maximum of £5,000 and or three months imprisonment. It is therefore essential; that the prospective buyer, ascertains the yacht's RCD status prior to entering into a contract with the seller.

For further detailed information on the RCD contact the RYA Technical Unit on 023 8060 4201.

RAISING THE MONEY

Most buyers will have to make arrangements to borrow the necessary funds from a bank, building society, finance house or some other source.

If the borrowing requirement is relatively modest (relative, that is, to the income of the purchaser) and it is expected to clear the debt quickly, a simple bank overdraft will usually be the most convenient option. If it is likely to take the buyer more than 12 months to pay the loan off, for amounts up to about £5000, a bank will usually try to sell a personal loan plan; for larger sums a variable loan rate, pegged to the bank's base rate, will be offered.

High street banks do not normally take mortgages over privately owned yachts, partly because the technicalities of registering a marine mortgage are outside their normal experience, and partly because the high cost of formal registration with the Registry of Shipping and Seamen and formal notification of the mortgage. For sums in excess of about £15,000 however, they may well look for a first or second charge over the borrower's house. A rate of 3½ to 4% above the base rate may be asked for a secured loan, although this is always open to negotiation particularly in periods of financial uncertainty when borrowers are in shorter supply than funds.

In recent years building societies have become very much more competitive in the personal loan market, and experience has shown that they can be more flexible when a borrower's cash flow makes it difficult to keep up the repayment schedule. This is not to say that funds should ever be borrowed without a clear idea of how the money is to be repaid, but financial uncertainties can disrupt the best laid plans and a supportive lender can often make the difference between survival and bankruptcy.

However the main players in the market are the specialist finance houses of which Lombard Marine Finance, Barclays Marine Finance and Bank of Scotland Marine are still the leaders, but with a number of other lenders who are often able to provide attractive deals.

The advantage of dealing with a specialist house is the availability of specific plans for marine finance and staff who are solely engaged in that area of business. When dealing with loans of £8,000 or more, the finance houses will generally take a mortgage over the yacht.

The additional security provided by the mortgage will enable them to offer an interest rate comparing favourably with a bank's unsecured loan rate. When lending £60,000 or more the finance house will insist on the yacht being registered on Part I of the the British Register.

Marine mortgage

Money has been raised on the security of ships for as long as there have been shipping and banking industries. The traditional method of mortgaging a ship (and the legal definition of ship includes "every description of vessel used in navigation") is by way of a formal charge on the Register of British Ships established under Part 1 of the 1995 Merchant Shipping Act. One of the main reasons for registering a yacht under the Part 1 Register, rather than the simpler and cheaper Small Ships Register, is to provide the basis for a formal mortgage to be arranged. No mortgage recording facility exists on the Small Ships Register.

The effect of a mortgage in favour of a financial institution is not to transfer ownership to the lender, but simply to restrict the borrower to using the yacht in a way that will not prejudice the lender's security. Thus the mortgage agreement will usually include clauses about chartering, lending, parting with possession, part sales of shares in the yacht, and of course insurance. In the case of a default in mortgage repayments the agreement will invariably allow the lender to repossess the yacht without any of the formalities, or protective provisions, that the owner of a private house may be entitled to.

Even after default and repossession however, the law allows the borrower an equitable right to redeem the security by paying off what is owing. In such a case the court will make an order directing that the accounts between parties should be finalised and that if the mortgagor fails to pay the sum due within a certain period (normally six months) then the mortgage will be foreclosed and the mortgagee (lender) will become the absolute owner of the property.

Unregistered mortgages

As we have seen, yachts registered on the Small Ships Register are not capable of being mortgaged under the procedures in the Merchant Shipping Acts. Although most financial institutions, particularly in the case of large mortgages on high value yachts, will insist on full Part 1 Registration and recording of a statutory mortgage, a number will now offer an unregistered mortgage facility to borrowers with very much less formality involved.

This form of unregistered mortgage is intended to provide the lender with a comparable degree of security to that provided under the Part 1 Register. Apart from the obvious cost advantage; (the requirement for Part 1 Registration would cost the borrower at least £500 in addition to the £105 mortgage registration fee, compared with a £12 registration fee for the Small Ships Register), an unregistered mortgage works in such a way as to vest actual title in the yacht to the lender. Arguably this is a better form of security for the lender than the simple charge allowed by a statutory mortgage, and lending rates for unregistered mortgages are generally no higher than for registered mortgages.

Repaying the mortgage

Although most finance houses are happy to allow terms of up to 5 years for cheaper craft, or up to 10 years at the top end of the market, some may attach penalties to mortgage agreements to discourage early settlement. Since this policy varies from one finance house to another, it will be worthwhile including this point when comparing rates from one company to another.

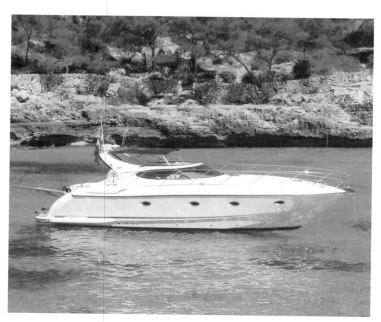

8 INSURANCE

Although yacht insurance in this country is not yet generally compulsory, there is so much scope for damage to the yacht, the crew, or other vessels in the ordinary course of navigation that it would be foolish not to have comprehensive insurance cover.

Unlike the simple form of contract used in household and motor car insurance, the standard yacht insurance policy is a complex document. It is difficult for the layman to understand the contract fully without access to the Marine Insurance Act 1906 and the body of marine insurance case law contained in the Lloyds law reports.

The yacht insurance market is highly competitive, divided between a number of Lloyds underwriters (who may be approached either through an agency or via Lloyds brokers) and insurance companies (who may be approached either through Lloyd's or non-Lloyd's brokers or direct). In the insurance market as anywhere else you get what you pay for, and while it is wise to shop around you should not be tempted to go for the underwriter or company offering the lowest premium for that reason alone. Experience has shown that underwriters and companies away from the cheaper end of the market tend to be more flexible in interpreting the strict terms of the policy in the case of difficult claims, and speedier in settling the more straightforward ones.

Also, since the 1994 European Directive on Unfair Terms in Consumer Contracts came into effect, most UK insurers have introduced new policy wordings to comply with the rule that contract wordings should be drafted in plain intelligible language. While this is to be generally welcomed, as the old Lloyd's Institute Yacht Clauses were difficult to interpret, the new approach has given rise to a wide variety of policy conditions, and while one insurer's cover may seem very much less expensive than another's, it may be that a close and expert comparison of the policy document will show the cheaper company to be offering very much more limited cover.

Although it may be going too far to say that the insurance market is using the requirement to re-write their policies into plain English as an excuse to narrow down the scope of cover intentionally, it is clear that this is the practical result of the new wordings in a number of cases. Before agreeing to insure his yacht under one of the new policies, a wise owner should ask his broker or underwriter to confirm in writing that the new policy will provide at least the same cover as that provided by the 1985 Lloyd's Institute Yacht Clauses.

When a broker is approached for a quotation, he will usually quote a figure between ½% and 1¼% of the declared value of the craft. There is always room for negotiation over premium rates, as the nature of risk varies according to a number of factors. Is the mooring secure against extremes of weather? Is the area patrolled by police or harbour officials to discourage vandalism and theft? What is the intended cruising range? Does the owner have any significant qualifications? Has the craft been built to current BW or NRA standards (and does the insurer regard that as relevant)? Is the owner prepared to carry a reasonable excess? (An agreement to pay the first £250 can make a big difference to the premium). Is the owner a member of a club that entitles him to a discount?

Most underwriters will be happy to insure a yacht up to 10 years old, without a survey being required. For older yachts a survey is usually required, and it will normally be a condition that the surveyor's major recommendations be implemented before full cover is given.

It is essential when completing the proposal form to put in the fullest and most accurate information and to answer all the questions literally. The proposal form constitutes the basis of a binding contract, and in the event of a claim, most underwriters will re-examine the proposal to ensure that the claim is valid within its terms of reference. The law recognises that insurance contracts are one-sided; the boatowner knows everything about himself, his boat and the nature of his proposed use of the boat. Since the insurer only knows what the owner chooses to tell him, he is protected by the principle of uberrima fides. Roughly translated this means that the insured must show the 'utmost good faith' in providing information, failure to do so will entitle the insurer to avoid the contract even if a subsequent claim is entirely irrelevant to the subject matter of the false statement.

So far as the average UK-based boatowner is concerned, there are three main cruising ranges available at standard prices which must be declared on a proposal form, these are:

(a)   non-tidal waters within the UK;

(b)   coastal cruising within an agreed range of the yacht's home port or permanent mooring;

(c) full coastal and sea-going cruising within the 'home trade' limits, which cover all UK waters and continental coasts from Brest to Elbe, (some policies may include continental inland ± waters as far south as Paris, but an additional premium is usually payable).

Particularly in the case of fast motorboats (insurers normally attach special conditions to boats capable of 17 knots or more) security against theft, or against the weather while at a mooring or at anchor is a major concern to insurers. They will usually insist that if a trailed boat is not kept at home, it must be made secure in a locked compound, and if left afloat unattended, must at all times be on a secure and reasonably sheltered mooring.

Unlike motor insurance, where the value of a car in the event of a write-off is taken to be its current market value, marine insurance is based on the principle of agreed value. If a yacht is insured for, say, £10,000, and in the case of total loss the insurers are able to show that it would have fetched no more than £8000 on the open market, they are still liable to pay the full figure. Provided the insured has not deliberately over stated the value, there should be no argument on the matter. This does not of course exempt him from accurately stating the price paid on the proposal form; this is not necessarily the same as the value of the yacht, although insurers may wish to know the reason for any difference in these figures.

Underwriters will of course need to be informed of any intention to use the yacht for charter, whether bareboat or skippered, or for any commercial purpose. While this is not a problem in itself, underwriters will normally lay down conditions about the qualifications and experience of prospective charterers.

Under the speedboat clauses in most policies, any use for racing or speed trials is specifically excluded, and special insurance should be taken out with the club organising any such event.

Difficulties can arise when an owner forgets to lay up (or re-launch) his yacht on the date stated on the proposal form. Claims have been turned down by underwriters on the grounds that the nature of risks while afloat are very different to those ashore. While most insurers are flexible about varying lay-up and relaunch dates, it is wise to inform them in advance of any proposed variation.

It is advisable to ensure that the policy offers cover, in an appropriate sum, for salvage claims.

So far as third party liability is concerned with effect from May 2004, most standard policies provide the owner with indemnity up to £2 or £3m. The RYA recommend a bare minimum of £2m. It should be remembered that such a high figure will rarely be approached, even in the case of a bad accident, as the Merchant Shipping Act Limitation of Liability provisions will normally apply. The effect of the limitation provisions is to allow a yacht owner (or his insurers) to limit liability for third-party property damage to about £360,000, and for death or personal injury to about £720,000. However, since limitation does not always apply in every circumstance, it is as well to carry substantial insurance against such misfortune.

An increasing number of harbour boards and navigation authorities are imposing third-party insurance requirements, and this trend is likely to continue over the next few years. In this context an important aspect of the cover provided is the cost of raising and removing the wreck of an insured boat in the event of it sinking in the fairway of a harbour or in the main channel of a navigable river or canal.

FINDING A MOORING_____

Much has been written in recent times about the shortage of mooring space in this country. This has been brought about by an increase of between 3 - 4,000 yachts built and imported each year, restrictive planning policies by local authorities controlling the development of new marinas, and the need of new yacht owners to find a mooring near large centres of population.

In fact there is ample space in our creeks, estuaries, rivers and harbours to provide moorings for two or three times the present numbers of small craft. The situation in certain defined areas is admittedly very tight; around the Solent space may be particularly expensive, but for those prepared to look a little further afield, to Poole, the Isle of Wight, along the Sussex coast or further West in Dorset there is much less pressure, with the further bonus of sailing in uncrowded waters.

Elsewhere around the coast many of the more popular small harbours have reached capacity, or unfairly restrict the grant of mooring licences to local residents. There will however always be space, and normally at a much lower cost, in the less accessible and less obvious areas and harbours. Unless you are intent on joining a keen racing fleet, or are very short of time to spend on travelling to your mooring, you should consider a mooring away from the most congested and expensive areas.

Looking further afield, many boat owners have chosen marina berths on the Mediterranean coasts of France and Spain, and claim that in doing so they are saving money and have more time for sailing. With cheap flights available from airports throughout the UK to areas with marina berthing available at one third to one quarter of the fees charged in the UK this can make a lot of sense, even taking into account the fact that VAT-free export to other EU States ceased to apply after 31st December 1992.

Owners wishing to keep their craft in a marina will find most of the options in the RYA *Marina Guide* published annually and on the RYA website. www.rya.org.uk

BUYING FOR USE ON INLAND WATERS

Although there have been construction and equipment regulations in force on the River Thames since the mid-1920's, regulations for privately-owned craft on waters controlled by British Waterways, the Norfolk and Suffolk Broads Authority and other Environment Agency waters (the Medway and Anglian rivers) are a very new concept, and will need to be complied with if it is intended to base a boat on those waters.

The two principal navigation authorities, have introduced a national Boat Safety Scheme (with effect from 1st January 1997) and have developed a training course and qualification scheme for inspectors. The intention is that a navigation licence or registration certificate will only be issued for craft that have a current certificate of compliance issued by an authorised inspector. If it is intended to base a boat on any BW or EA waters, compliance with the scheme will be compulsory.

Details of the scheme are available on request from:

British Waterways
Willow Grange
Church Road
WATFORD
WD1 3QA

Tel: 01923 226422

Environment Agency
Recreation and Navigation
Rio House
Waterside Drive
Aztec West
Almondsbury
BRISTOL
BS12 4UD

Tel: 01454 624376

BUYING FOR COMMERCIAL USE ___

Reference has been made to regulations established by the Department for Transport for commercially-used pleasure craft. Most of the Merchant Shipping legislation laying down rules for the design, construction and equipment of ships specifically exempts pleasure yachts or pleasure craft from compliance. However the Marques incident in 1985, in which a converted trading schooner capsized and sank with serious loss of life in a Tall Ships Race, led to the DfT amending the rules to exclude commercially used yachts from exemption, and to require them to comply with a stringent Code of Practice. The regulations have been in force since 1994.

Yachts used bona fide for the private pleasure of an owner or his family or friends, or within a club syndicate, are exempt, provided that any contribution to costs is for running expenses only. Any charters, whether crewed or bare-boat, will bring a yacht within the regulations, (unless the charter is primarily for racing purposes), and indeed any other commercial purpose will also necessitate compliance with the Code of Practice.

The regulations cover various areas of operation, in 5 categories from less than 20 miles from a safe haven, to unrestricted service, and encompass all aspects of design and equipment, including stability requirements, weathertightness, requirement for diesel engine, detailed electrical arrangements, fire prevention requirements, and lifesaving and safety equipment.

Many of these requirements will certainly be expensive to comply with, and undoubtedly go far beyond what has conventionally been considered adequate for cruising yachts in the past. Any prospective owner considering subsidising his costs by occasional chartering (let alone running the yacht on a full-time charter basis) should study the Code of Practice in detail and draw up detailed costings of the additional construction and equipment requirements, before entering into a binding contract to buy the yacht.

Details of the Code of Practice for craft up to 24 metres can be obtained from:

Maritime and Coastguard Agency
Spring Place, 105 Commercial Road
Southampton SO15 1EG

Tel: 023 8032 9100

APPENDIX I

AGREEMENT FOR THE SALE AND PURCHASE OF A SECONDHAND YACHT

An agreement prepared by the Royal Yachting Association for the sale of a secondhand yacht between persons not normally engaged in the business of selling yachts.

AN AGREEMENT made the.........day of............20..............

BETWEEN :

1. 'The Vendor' :

of

2. 'The Purchaser' :

of

The terms "Vendor" and "Purchaser" include their respective successors in title and the Vendor and Purchaser shall hereinafter be collectively referred to as "the Parties".

'The Purchase Price' : £.......................sterling

'The Deposit' ....: 10% of the Purchase Price

In respect of the sale of a [REGISTERED/UNREGISTERED] PLEASURE CRAFT

Name :

Description :

Official No. :

Port of Registry where applicable :

Hull Identification Number

Now lying at :

Including all equipment, machinery and gear on board ('the Yacht') and any specific inventory attached hereto initialled by the Parties and forming part of this Agreement.

1. Agreement for sale

The Vendor hereby agrees to sell and the Purchaser agrees to purchase the Yacht free from any encumbrances (subject to the conditions and terms of this agreement), together with all her outfit gear and equipment as set out in a schedule hereto but not including stores or the Vendor's personal effects, for the Purchase Price.

2. Payment of deposit

On the signing of this agreement the Deposit is to be paid to the Vendor and the balance of the Purchase Price together with any Value Added Tax shall be payable in accordance with Clause 6.

3.1 Value Added Tax

The price is inclusive of any VAT or Customs Duty which may be payable by the Seller.

[If the Vendor is a registered person for the purpose of VAT or if the price is not inclusive of VAT or any Tax or Duty other appropriate terms should agreed and recorded regarding responsibility for their payment].

3.2 Import dues and local taxes (craft lying overseas)

The Vendor warrants that the craft has been properly imported into [   ] and that all appropriate local taxes and dues have been paid and that the proposed sale is in accordance with all relevant local laws and regulations.

4. Inspection survey

The Purchaser may, at a venue to be agreed and at his own cost, haul out or place ashore and/or open up the Yacht and her machinery for the purposes of inspection and/or survey which, including any written report, shall be completed within fourteen days of the signing of this agreement. If any inspection requires more than superficial non-destructive dismantling the consent of the Vendor must be obtained before such work commences.

5.1 Notice of defects

Within seven days after receipt of a report following such inspection and/or survey if any material defect(s) in the Yacht or her machinery other than disclosed to the Purchaser in writing prior to the signing of this agreement or any material deficiencies in her inventory, if any, shall have been found the Purchaser may either :

5.1.1

give notice to the Vendor of his rejection of the Yacht provided that the notice shall specify any material defect(s) or deficiencies; or

5.1.2

give notice to the Vendor specifying any material defect(s) or deficiencies and requiring the Vendor forthwith either to make good the same or make a sufficient reduction in the Purchase Price to enable the Purchaser to make good the same. All agreed items of work to be completed without undue delay in all circumstances and to be carried out so as to satisfy the expressly specified requirements of the Purchaser's surveyor in respect only of material defects mentioned in his report and specified in the notice to the Vendor.

5.2

If the Purchaser shall have served a notice of rejection under Clause 5.1.1, then this agreement shall be deemed to be rescinded forthwith and the Vendor shall refund to the purchaser the Deposit in accordance with Clause 8.

5.3

If the Purchaser shall have served a notice under Clause 5.1.2 requiring the Vendor to make good material defects or deficiencies or to make a reduction in the Purchase Price, and the Vendor shall not have agreed within twenty one days after the service of the notice to make good such defects or the Parties have not agreed in the twenty one days after the service of notice upon the reduction in the Purchase Price, then this agreement shall be deemed to have been rescinded on the twenty second day after the service of notice and the Vendor shall refund to the Purchaser the Deposit in accordance with Clause 8.

In the case of any deficiencies in the Yacht's inventory (if any) remaining or arising within seven days of acceptance in accordance with Clause 6 the deficiencies shall be made good or a reduction in the Purchase Price shall be agreed, failing which this agreement shall be rescinded at the option of the Purchaser only.

6.1 Acceptance of yacht

The Yacht shall be deemed to have been accepted by the Purchaser and the balance of the Purchase Price and any Value Added Tax thereon shall become due and payable in accordance with Clause 7 upon the happening of any of the following events :

6.2

The expiry of fourteen days from the date of this agreement or such extended period as may be agreed between the Parties provided that no inspection or survey has been commenced;

6.3

The expiry of eight days from the receipt of a report following a survey, and/or inspection provided that the Purchaser has not served notice under Clause 5.1;

6.4

Notification in writing by the Vendor to the Purchaser of completion of the remedial works specified in a notice given by the Purchaser under Clause 5.1.2;

7.1 Completion of sale

Upon acceptance of the Yacht by the Purchaser, the Deposit shall be treated as part payment of the Purchase Price. Within seven days of acceptance the Purchaser shall pay the balance of the Purchase Price and any Value Added Tax thereon and the Vendor shall :

In the case of a registered yacht

7.1.1 Registered yacht

provide the Purchaser with the Certificate of Registry, correct and updated, together with any other documents appertaining to the Yacht and shall execute a Bill of Sale, in the prescribed form, in favour of the Purchaser or his nominee, showing the Yacht to be free from encumbrances and completed so as to ensure transfer on the Register;

OR

7.1.2 In the case of an unregistered yacht (including a yacht registered on the SSR)

(a) Provide the Purchaser with a Bill of Sale in favour of the Purchaser or his nominee, together with any other documents appertaining to the Yacht;

(b) Deliver to the Purchaser any necessary delivery order or other authority enabling the Purchaser to take immediate possession of the Yacht.

7.2

Where payment is made by cheque, draft, letter of credit or other instrument, the terms of this agreement shall not be deemed to have been fulfilled until such payment is cleared into the payee's account.

7.3 Vendor's right to assign title

By delivery of the documents specified in either case the Vendor shall be deemed to have covenanted AND HEREBY COVENANTS that he has the right to transfer property in the Yacht and that the same is free from all encumbrances, debts, liens and the like except such encumbrances and liabilities for duties, taxes, debts, liens and the like as are the responsibility of the Purchaser under Clauses 4 and 8.

7.4 Free access after completion

On completion, the Vendor shall ensure that the Yacht is available for collection by the Purchaser and that free access by the Purchaser together with all necessary haulage equipment is permitted at no additional cost to the Purchaser.

8.1 Rescission of agreement

In the event of rescission of this agreement by the Purchaser he shall, at his own expense, reinstate the Yacht to the condition and position in which he found her, and shall pay all boatyard and surveyor's charges for this work.

8.2 Return of deposit

The Vendor shall thereupon return the Deposit to the Purchaser without deduction and without interest save that he shall be entitled to retain such part of the Deposit as shall be necessary to defray any boatyard or surveyor's charges not paid by the Purchaser.

Neither party shall thereafter have any claim against the other under this agreement.

9. Warranties

The Vendor being a person not selling the Yacht in the course of a business, and the Purchaser being at liberty to inspect the Yacht and satisfy himself as to her condition and specification, all express or implied warranties or conditions, statutory or otherwise, are hereby excluded and the Yacht, her outfit, gear and equipment shall be taken with all defects and faults of description without any allowance or abatement whatsoever.

10. Risk

Until the Yacht has been accepted or shall be deemed to have been accepted by the Purchaser she shall be at the risk of the Vendor who shall make good all damage sustained by her before the date of acceptance. If the Yacht be lost or becomes a constructive total loss before such acceptance, this agreement shall be null and void except that the Purchaser will be liable for the cost of all work authorised by him under Clauses 4 and 8 and undertaken before such loss took place and the Deposit shall be returned to the Purchaser without interest but less any deduction made under Clauses 4 and 8 and otherwise without deduction and the Purchaser shall have no claim against the Vendor for damages or otherwise. After acceptance the Yacht shall in all respects be at the risk of the Purchaser.

Notwithstanding the provisions of this clause the ownership of the Yacht will not vest in the Purchaser until payment of the balance of the Purchase Price in accordance with Clause 7 even though the Purchaser may have insured his risk under the provisions of this clause.

11.1 Default by purchaser

Should the Purchaser fail to pay the balance of the Purchase Price in accordance with Clause 7, the Vendor may give notice in writing to the Purchaser requiring him to complete the purchase within fourteen days of the service of such notice.

If the Purchaser fails to comply with the notice then the Vendor may re-sell the Yacht by public auction or private treaty and any deposit paid shall thereupon be forfeit without prejudice to the Vendor's right to claim from the Purchaser the amount of any loss on re-sale together with all his reasonable costs and expenses, due allowance being made for any forfeited deposit. On the expiry of the said notice the Yacht shall be at the Vendor's risk.

11.2 Default by vendor

If the Vendor shall default in the execution of his part of the contract the Purchaser shall, without prejudice to any other rights he may have hereunder, be entitled to the return of the Deposit.

Unless such default by the Vendor shall have arisen from events over which the Vendor had no control, the Vendor shall pay interest upon the amount of the Deposit for the period during which he has held it at the rate of 4% per annum above finance house base rate, together with compensation for any loss which the Purchaser may have sustained as a result of the Vendor's default.

12. Arbitration

All disputes that cannot be resolved between the Parties and which arise out of or in connection with this agreement shall be submitted to a single arbitrator to be appointed, in default of agreement, by the Chief Executive of the RYA and the provisions of the Arbitration Act 1950 (as amended) shall apply.

13. Notices

Any notice under this agreement shall be in writing and any notice to the Purchaser or Vendor shall be sufficiently served if delivered to him personally or posted by recorded delivery to his last known address. Any notice posted shall be deemed to have been received forty eight hours after the time of posting and any notice given in any other manner shall be deemed to have been received at the time when, in the ordinary course of post, it may be expected to have been received.

14. Jurisdiction

This agreement shall be construed according to, and governed by the Law of England (or of Scotland if the Vendor's address shall be in that country) and the Parties hereby submit to the jurisdiction of the Courts of the same countries.

15. Marginal notes

The construction of this agreement is not to be affected by any marginal notes.

16. Rights under contract or statute

This agreement forms the entire agreement between the Parties unless otherwise specifically agreed in writing between them.

SIGNED BY THE VENDOR

In the presence of :

SIGNED BY THE PURCHASER

In the presence of :

APPENDIX 2

AGREEMENT FOR THE SYNDICATE OWNERSHIP OF A YACHT

AN AGREEMENT made the...............day of ....20...........

BETWEEN.........................of.....................................

('the first owner')

and...............................of.......................................

('the second owner')

The owners include their respective successors in title and shall hereinafter be collectively referred to as 'the Parties'.

WHEREAS the Parties wish to enter into an agreement to share the management and use of the yacht .... (the Yacht)

[and WHEREAS the first owner is the present owner of the Yacht]

[and WHEREAS the second owner has by a prior contract purchased from the first owner /64ths of the Yacht]

[and WHEREAS the Parties have jointly and severally purchased the Yacht in the following shares :

   the first owner purchasing   /64ths

   the second owner purchasing   /64ths

[and WHEREAS the parties have jointly and severally entered into

an agreement with [   ] (the 'Mortgage Company')].

NOW IT IS HEREBY MUTUALLY AGREED between the Parties as follows :

1.   Joint bank account

The first owner shall forthwith open a [Bank/ Building Society] account ('the Account') in the names of the Parties into which the Parties shall upon the [   ] day of [   ] in each year transfer the amount of £[   ] until six months after the termination of this agreement in accordance with Clause 5.

2.   Withdrawals and contributions from/to account

The first [and second] owner/s shall have power [jointly/separately] to draw monies from the Account for the sole purpose of the maintenance and management of the

Yacht as [he/they] shall in their absolute discretion think fit and shall have power to call for further and necessary contributions in equal shares from [the second owner/each other] subject always to the safeguards in Clause 4.7 and to the general law affecting principal and agent.

3. Casual disbursements

Any disbursement, payment or account discharged by one owner on behalf of the other and of the general management of the yacht shall from time to time as convenient but certainly once annually be reported to the other owner and each owner jointly and severally agrees to contribute one half of such disbursements, payments or accounts upon proper documentation in the form of receipts, etc. being presented as evidence of payment.

4. Management responsibility

The first owner shall have the following powers, duties and responsibilities :

4.1

to make day-to-day decisions for the general management of the Yacht;

4.2

to make (after consultation with the second owner) any arrangement for the purchase of capital equipment such as sails, engines etc. as may be necessary and for any agreement to charter the Yacht;

4.3

to insure the Yacht, her apparel, fittings etc. against the usual risks either at Lloyds or with an insurance company or association;

4.4

to employ any yard, sail-loft, brokers or agents on their usual terms of business and to transact any necessary business in relation to the Yacht;

4.5

to make, adjust, apportion or settle at his discretion any salvage, damage, average or other claims in favour of or against the Yacht or to refer the same to arbitration;

4.6

to take such steps as may be necessary to defend proceedings, accept service or arrange finance relating to the Yacht;

4.7

as soon as reasonably practicable after the [   ] day of [   ] in each year to render to the second owner accounts paid together with the Account statements as evidence of payment, and on request to produce all vouchers, books or other documents and papers relating to the management of the Account and of the Yacht.

5. Termination of agreement

If either of the Parties has reasonable cause or desire to terminate this agreement, he may, by individual notice in writing to the other party, indicate his desire to terminate. Such termination shall take place within six months after the delivery of such notice in writing.

Upon such notice in writing being delivered, the other party shall take such steps as may be necessary to secure the execution of a proper release and indemnity against all liabilities contracted by the determining party and shall arrange to purchase the share of the determining party at a fair market price or alternatively obtain agreement by another to take on the share of the determining party. Likewise, the determining party hereby agrees to defray or settle all his share of the disbursements, payments or accounts for the Yacht up to and including the date of actual termination as agreed between the Parties which for the avoidance of doubt may be any date within six months of the individual notice in writing being received by the other party.

If a dispute arises as to the price to be paid to the determining party for his share then a valuation shall be obtained from a recognised yacht broker and in default of agreement then the entirety of the Yacht shall be publicly advertised for sale with notice of time and place for sale being given to both Parties and she shall be sold. Each of the Parties on receiving his share of the purchase money shall execute the necessary Bill of Sale of his share in the Yacht to the purchaser and deliver up possession of the Yacht. The costs of such sale shall be paid by the Parties according to their respective shares.

6.

Where it is agreed to terminate this agreement and the Parties have mutually agreed to sell the Yacht, it shall then be sold either by private treaty at such price as the Parties may agree or, in default of such agreement, by public auction subject to such conditions as are usual on the sale of such yachts. Each of the Parties shall be at liberty to bid for and purchase the Yacht at any such public auction, or to purchase the Yacht outright for the price advertised for sale by private treaty.

7.1 Regular payment of mortgage etc.

In the case of a mortgage or hire purchase agreement being in operation each owner jointly and severally agrees to pay his monthly or other contribution to defray the costs of such mortgage or hire purchase agreement into the Account in accordance with Clause 1 until the date of determination agreed in accordance with Clause 5.

7.2 Final settlement of mortgage debt

In the event of the sale of the Yacht, each owner jointly and severally agrees with the other to defray from his share of the sale price his share of the mortgage or hire purchase agreement entered into with the Mortgage Company.

8. Arbitration

If any dispute, difference or question arises between the Parties relating to the rights, duties or obligations of either of them, including (without prejudice to the generality hereof) any dispute, difference or question whether the owners have, in fact, properly and satisfactorily carried out their obligations under this agreement, the same shall be referred to arbitration by a single arbitrator to be agreed upon by the Parties or, failing such agreement, appointed by the Chief Executive of the RYA.
This shall be deemed to be a submission to arbitration within the Arbitration Acts.

9.

Any notice under this agreement shall be in writing and shall be sufficiently served if delivered personally or posted to the last known postal address in Great Britain or Ireland of either of the Parties.

IN WITNESS whereof this agreement has been signed by the Parties the day and year first above written

SIGNED BY THE FIRST OWNER

in the presence of :

SIGNED BY THE SECOND OWNER

in the presence of :

APPENDIX 3

ABYA CODE OF PRACTICE FOR THE SALE OF USED BOATS (Refer to ABYA for updates)

SECTION FOUR

BROKER AND VENDOR/PURCHASER

1. ### Legal liability to disclose information

   (i) Vendors

   Brokers must incorporate into 'instructions to sell' forms and/or particulars/questionnaire forms, a clause to the effect:

   'The Vendor declares that to the best of his knowledge and belief the particulars given to the broker and signed or supplied by the Vendor are correct, and that he has power to dispose of the vessel with the concurrence of any joint owner or mortgagee or hire purchase company and all known defects have been declared and that he understands the implications of the Misrepresentations Act of 1976 and agrees to indemnify the Broker against all costs, claims and demands arising in consequence of any of the information given in the particulars being incorrect.'

   (ii) Brokers

   The Broker is responsible for providing accurate information to the best of his ability, and defects or deficiencies in a boat of which the Broker is aware must be divulged to Purchasers and the Vendor. (See paragraph 2 (iii) of Section 3)

2. ### Central agencies (Sole Agents)

   Central Agency instructions from Vendors must be in writing and must be produced by the Central Agent on request of another Member. If a Vendor states his intention of appointing only one agent, but reserves the right to sell his boat privately, this is not a Central Agency.

3. ### Offers

   In the absence of express agreement to the contrary, the Vendor's approval to sell must be obtained even when the asking price has been offered and all offers must be submitted until such time as a deposit acceptable to the Vendor is paid and the terms agreed by the Vendor.

4. Contract

An Agreement for the Sale and Purchase of a Second Hand Yacht on a recognised ABYA approved form should always be used, but, in the absence of such an agreement, it is recommended that Brokers establish a contract in the form of a receipt or otherwise by memorandum. Such receipt or memorandum should state that any deposit paid is deemed to be held on the terms of the said ABYA approved form.

5. Quoted prices

Brokers must not offer boats at a lower figure than that quoted by the Vendor. The price quoted shall be in all cases the gross price inclusive of commission. Where applicable, any VAT liability must be indicated in accordance with current legislation.

6. Surveys

Other than in exceptional circumstances, a Broker should always advise a Purchaser to have a survey. However, a Broker should not recommend a particular surveyor but may accept the Purchaser's instructions to appoint a surveyor on his behalf. On no account shall the Broker make or receive a commission in connection with the survey.

7. Sale proceeds

The Broker shall be responsible for keeping the deposit, part payments and the proceeds of the sale in a separate banking account designated for the purpose, and shall account for the same to the Vendor after deducting such commission as may be properly due to the Broker or his Sharing Broker within fourteen days of the sale being effected, or where applicable after transfer of clear title to the Purchaser, whichever shall be later.

8. Title and registration

At the time of the sale the Lead Broker shall obtain evidence of title a properly executed Bill of Sale or receipt showing the boat to be free from encumbrances, which shall be exchanged for the cleared purchase monies for the boat. Brokers are required to provide the facility, at a reasonable extra charge, to their clients for dealing with British Registration procedures and Customs Documentation.

*(Practice Note: While a Purchaser or Vendor is not obliged to engage a Broker to transfer ownership of a registered vessel, the Broker is strongly advised to encourage the Purchaser and Vendor to appoint him for this purpose, and it is recommended that only modest fees be charged for this service on order to encourage continuity of Registration.)

9. Standard disclaimer for particulars

It is recommended that the following wording is included in any particulars shown to a prospective purchaser.

'In this case we are acting as Brokers only. The Vendor is/is not selling in the course of business. [Delete as necessary.]

Whilst every care has been taken in their preparation, the correctness of these particulars is not guaranteed. The particulars are intended only as a guide and they do not constitute a term of any contract. A prospective buyer is strongly advised to check the particulars and where appropriate, at his own expense to employ a qualified marine surveyor to carry out a survey and/or to have an engine trial conducted.'

*(Practice Note: This disclaimer will not be appropriate in all circumstances and care should be taken to ensure that it is suitably amended and/or deleted as necessary, for example; in the case where the Broker is acting as a principal; where the Vendor is selling in the course of business; where VAT is payable; if an engine is not fitted and so on.)

APPENDIX 4

Marine Finance Houses in BMF Membership

Lombard Marine Finance
371 Millbrook Road West
Southampton, Hampshire
SO15 0HW

Tel: 023 8051 5050

Barclays Marine Finance
Saltmakers House
Hamble Point Marina
School Lane, Hamble
Southampton SO31 4NB

Tel: 0800 445644

Bank of Scotland Marine
Alleyn House
23/27 Carlton Crescent
Southampton, Hampshire
SO15 2RB

Tel: 023 8033 3467

APPENDIX 5

Bill of Sale

for the Yacht ....('the Yacht')

Type: ....

Year built: ....

Length: ....

Beam: ....

Auxiliary Power: ....

Small Ships Reg. No: ....

Hull Identification Number ....

I/we .... [and ....

of: .... of: ....

....]

('the Transferor[s]')

IN CONSIDERATION of the sum of £........................

(.............................. pounds) paid to me/us by:

.... [and ....

of: .... of: ....

....]

('the Transferee[s]')

receipt of which is acknowledged;

1. **Transfer** the Yacht to the Transferee[s];
2. For myself/ourselves and for my/our heirs **covenant** with the Transferee[s] and his/their heirs and assigns that I/we have power so to transfer and that the Yacht is free from encumbrances.

SIGNED this.................day of .... 20[   ]

.... (signature of Transferor[s])

[.......................]

in the presence of:

....

.... (signature of Witness)

.... (name of Witness)

of: .... (address of Witness)

Notes:

1. This form of Bill of Sale is produced by the RYA for use by Personal Members for the transfer of an un-registered yacht or a yacht registered on the Part III (Small Ships) Register. Transfers of yachts registered under Part 1 of the 1995 Merchant Shipping Act should be evidenced using the Bill of Sale prescribed by The Registry of Shipping and Seamen, PO Box 420, Cardiff, CF24 5XR.

2. Please delete inapplicable alternatives.

3. This form of Bill of Sale should not be used when transfer is by gift, or if any of the parties to it is a corporate body.

4. Separate copies of this draft Bill of Sale (in A4 format) are available to **personal members of the RYA** on request.

APPENDIX 6

Useful addresses and telephone numbers

British Marine Federation
Marine House
Thorpe Lea Road, Egham
Surrey TW20 8BF

Tel: 01784 473377

Registry of Shipping and Seamen
P.O. Box 420
Cardiff CF24 5XR

Tel: 02920 448800

Royal Yachting Association
RYA House, Ensign Way
Hamble, Southampton
SO31 4YA

Tel: 0845 345 0400

Yacht Brokers, Designers and Surveyors Association
The Glass Works
Penns Road
Petersfield, Hampshire
GU32 2EW

Tel: 01730 710425

HM Customs and Excise

VAT enquiry line 0845 010 9000

APPENDIX 7_____

Taxation rates in EU states as at May 2004

AUSTRIA   VAT at 20%

CYPRUS   VAT at 15%

CZECH REPUBLIC   VAT at 22%

BELGIUM   VAT 21% on new or imported boats. "First
                  Registration" tax of 25M) ECU payable on new
                  boats above 7.5m. Registration tax of 2500 ECU
                  decreasing by 10% per annum payable on
                  resale.

DENMARK   VAT payable on full value of boat when dealer is
                  involved in transaction in force. VAT rate 25%.
                  Light and navaid tax based on 1% of insurance
                  value in force.

ESTONIA   VAT at 18%

FINLAND   VAT at 22%.

FRANCE   VAT at 19.6%. Tax on all users of inland
                  waterways under consideration. Annual user tax
                  based on engine power greater than 5hp and
                  hull size (greater than 3GRT) in force.

GERMANY   Tax on dealer's margin in force. VAT on new
                  boats 16% in force.

GREECE   VAT at 18%

HUNGARY	VAT at 25%
IRELAND	VAT at 21%.
ITALY	VAT at 20%
LATVIA	VAT at 18%
LITHUANIA	VAT at 18%
LUXENBOURG	VAT at 15%
MALTA	VAT at 18%
NETHERLANDS	VAT at 19%
POLAND	VAT at 22%.
PORTUGAL	VAT at 19% for all types of boats. Annual tax depending on length and engine power.
SLOVAKIA	VAT at 19%
SLOVENIA	VAT at 20%
SPAIN	VAT at 16% on all boats plus a 13% registration tax on boats over 7.5m. This is compulsory for Spanish nationals and to all others who wish to register their boat in Spain.
SWEDEN	VAT at 25%
UK	VAT at 17.5%

APPENDIX 8

VAT Guide for Yachts issued by HM Customs and Excise (Not including Channel Islands, Malta or Gibraltar)

This leaflet is for UK yachtsmen who still have concerns about VAT when cruising in the EU or when returning from outside the EU.

Vessels purchased/acquired within the EU

UK residents should only use a boat in the Community if it is VAT paid, or 'deemed' VAT paid. Documentary evidence supporting this should be carried at all times.

- Original invoice or receipt

- Evidence that VAT was paid at importation

If the vessel was in use as a private pleasure craft before 1/1/1985 and was in the EU on 31/12/1992, it may be 'deemed' VAT paid under an age-related relief. Documentary evidence to support this could be:

For age

- Marine Survey • Part I Registration

- Insurance Documents • Builder's Certificate

For location at 31/12/92

- Receipt for mooring • Receipt for Harbour Dues

- Dry dock records

As Austria, Finland and Sweden joined the Single Market two years later, the relevant dates will be... in use before 1/1/1987 and moored in EU on 31/12/1994.

Other documents which could demonstrate VAT status could be: Evidence that Returned Goods Relief (RGR) has been granted Evidence that Transfer of Residence Relief (TOR) has been granted (Subject to one year restriction on disposal).

In the absence of any of the above, whilst cruising within the EU you should carry a Bill of Sale (between two private individuals in the UK). Whilst this is not conclusive proof that VAT has been paid, it does indicate that tax status is the responsibility of UK Customs.

Vessels purchased/acquired outside the EU

Any yacht purchased outside the EU will be liable for VAT, regardless of age or previous tax history. There may also be Import Duty unless the vessel is more than 12m overall or built in the EU. Charges become due at the first port of call within the EU (See Public Notice No 3).

Buying a new vessel in one member state of the EU to take to another

Yachts purchased NEW within the EU pay VAT at the country of destination. For example, if you buy a new yacht in France, you should send appendix D of Public Notice No 728 to the local Customs & Excise office within 7 days of arrival in the UK.

Buying a vessel in the UK for export from the EU

You can purchase a vessel tax free if you intend to export it, under it's own power to a destination outside the EU. Full details can be found in VAT leaflet 703/3/98.

Voyages outside the EU

Part 1 of form C1331 should be lodged with Customs prior to departure if you are going directly to a country outside the EU, ie Channel Islands, Malta and Gibraltar etc. On return to the UK you should report your arrival as per Public Notice No.8 page 6.

For further information contact, your local Advice Centre, or look in your phone book Under Customs & Excise.

APPENDIX 9

The VAT guide must now be read in line with the accession on 1st May 2004 of the new 10 EU Member States; namely, Cyprus, Czech Republic, Estonia, Hungary, Latvia, Lithuania, Malta, Poland, Slovakia and Slovenia.

In terms of the Age Related Relief exemption, the transitional period for the new Member States is as follows:

The vessel must have been in use as a private pleasure craft on 1st May 1996 and moored in EU waters on 30th April 2004.

The documentary evidence in support of this exemption is the same as for all other EU Member States.

The reference to Malta being excluded from the VAT regulations in Appendix 8 is no longer applicable.

For further advice on VAT issues, contact Customs and Excise on 0845 010 9000.

Devon Aerodromes

IN OLD PHOTOGRAPHS

KEITH A. SAUNDERS

Alan Sutton Publishing Limited
Phoenix Mill · Far Thrupp · Stroud
Gloucestershire

First Published 1994

For George Raby (1944–1989),
a valued friend

British Library Cataloguing in Publication Data.
A catalogue record for this book is available from
the British Library.

ISBN 0-7509-0808-4

Typeset in 9/10 Sabon.
Typesetting and origination by
Alan Sutton Publishing Limited.
Printed in Great Britain by
Hartnolls, Bodmin, Cornwall.

Contents

Introduction

Historians state that manned flight in Devon dates to the nineteenth century, when hot-air balloons were launched from both Plymouth Hoe and the Castle Yard in Exeter. However, a new century would dawn before the populace of the county would hold its breath, while the pioneers of heavier-than-air flight demonstrated their flimsy flying machines at Torquay and Exeter. In the fifty years that followed Devon would play host to a variety of airmen and flying machines, mirroring the first half-century of worldwide aeronautical achievement.

During July 1910, the Royal Navy assembled its fleets in Torbay for review by King George V and Queen Mary. More than 150 warships were anchored off Torquay when pioneer aviator Claude Grahame-White, watched by incredulous crowds, lifted his early biplane from the grass in front of Torre Abbey and flew briefly above the ships. Whether the Admiralty perceived the future vulnerability of warships to air attack is unrecorded.

The second demonstration occurred at Exeter, just twelve months later, when competitors in the 1,010-mile Circuit of Britain landed at the compulsory control stop at Arena Park. Racing for the £10,000 offered by the *Daily Mail*, the course was flown over five days with thirteen compulsory control stops. Nationally the contest aroused a great deal of public interest with large crowds of spectators and groups of schoolchildren welcoming the fliers to Exeter. The eventual winner was Lt. Jean Conneau of the French Navy, racing as 'Beaumont' and taking 22 hr 28 min to complete the course at an average speed of 45 mph.

Saltram Park, Plymouth and the South Molton Agricultural Show would also welcome the early aviators, while Knightshayes Court at Tiverton would provide a flying field for Henri Salmet, the famed French flier, during his *Daily Mail*-sponsored tour of Devon and Cornwall during June 1912.

The First World War and the threat to shipping from enemy submarines saw squadrons of the Royal Naval Air Service operating small airships and fixed-wing aircraft in anti-submarine and reconnaissance roles from bases at the Cattewater, Laira, Prawle Point, Torquay and Westward Ho! The Armistice saw all but the first-named relinquish military flying activities.

Cattewater would in turn be renamed RAF Mount Batten on 1 October 1929, with the incumbent squadrons operating Saro Londons, Blackburn Irises, Supermarine Scapas and Southamptons from the station during the inter-war years.

During the hostilities that followed between 1939 and 1945, Mount Batten initially hosted the Sunderland I flying boats of 204 Squadron but it is with the aircrews of 10 Squadron, Royal Australian Air Force, that the station will always be associated. Operating over the Bay of Biscay and Western Approaches, under the direction of 19 Group, Coastal Command, 10 Squadron would undertake 3,177 sorties and sink seven U-boats before returning home in October 1945. Losses included nineteen Sunderlands to enemy action and a further six in flying accidents.

Returning to the First World War, when the Armistice was agreed in November 1918, official restrictions on civil flying were not lifted, since a state of war technically existed until the signing of the peace treaty in July 1919. Meanwhile a Civil Aviation Department was formed within the Air Ministry on 12 February 1919, with Winston Churchill being appointed Secretary of State for Air, with authority to prepare supplementary air traffic regulations that would incorporate airworthiness and registration requirements.

Prior to the bill becoming law in October 1919, provision was made for the resumption of civil flying in accordance with the regulations set out in the Air Navigation Bill, and British civil aviation officially came into existence on 1 May.

Entrepreneurs quickly recognized a huge market of people wanting to experience flight and this need was met by the 'barnstormers'. A.V. Roe and Co. Ltd established the Avro Transport Company to meet public demand and during 1919 operated a small fleet of Avro 504L seaplanes from the Isle of Wight resorts, Hayling Island and Paignton's Preston beach. Flights along the Devon coast to Torquay and Teignmouth were popular, with 250 passengers carried during August and September 1919.

Elsewhere in the county, cities and towns were visited by the joyriding operations of the East Hanney-based Berkshire Aviation Company of F.J.V. and J.D.V. Holmes and the St Austell-based Cornwall Aviation Company of Captain Percival Phillips. Both organizations operated the ubiquitous Avro 504K with the red biplanes of the Cornish company later joining the National Aviation Day tour of Alan Cobham that would in turn visit West Country towns.

Civil flying found a more permanent base when, on 6 May 1928, William Richard Parkhouse landed his new Avro Avian biplane on Haldon Moor and towed it to Teignmouth for display in the showrooms of his motor and agricultural business.

An aerodrome was quickly established at Little Haldon with flying instruction and regular flying meetings taking place. An early pupil was the sixteen-year-old Whitney Straight, who flew solo from Haldon on his seventeenth birthday and was destined to become managing director of the British Overseas Airways Corporation. Haldon would later feature in the pre-war schedules of GWR Air Services, Railway Air Services and Provincial Airways.

During the Second World War, Haldon was used as a satellite by the Fighter School at Yeovilton, for Fleet Air Arm target tugs operating over the Lyme Bay gunnery ranges. Air Training Corps gliders were also accommodated. After the war, Haldon quickly faded into obscurity.

Also opened for flying activities during 1928 was the early RAF airfield at Folley Gate, near Okehampton. Opened each summer thereafter, the grass airfield was used by the Army Cooperation aircraft of 13 and 16 Squadrons operating in conjunction with artillery practice camps on the Dartmoor ranges.

During the late summer of 1940, 16 Squadron based its Lysanders at Okehampton, flying coastal patrols from dawn to dusk. Further wartime use continued in support of the Dartmoor ranges before the site became a forward holding unit for aircraft spares. As 1944 drew to a close, US Army Piper Cubs resided briefly at the airfield. During the 1950s, AOP Austers were infrequent visitors to Okehampton when operating in support of the artillery ranges.

Despite having first been used for flying as early as 1923, it was not until 15 July 1931 that Roborough Airport at Plymouth was officially opened. Incorporating the Polo Ground and surrounding fields, the airport, like Haldon, featured in the schedules of domestic airlines including Railway Air Services and Provincial Airways, the latter operating a service between Croydon, Portsmouth, Christchurch, Haldon and Plymouth.

The war years followed, first under Admiralty control and from May 1942 under the control of the Air Ministry. During the Battle of Britain period obsolete Gladiator biplanes of 247 Squadron guarded the dockyard, but it was in the communications and anti-aircraft cooperation roles that Roborough saw out the war before the resumption of civil flying in 1946, being operated by the Plymouth and District Aero Club (Straight Corporation) on behalf of the City Council. The DH Rapides of Jersey Airlines commenced services to Plymouth during 1952, being joined by other operators whose tenure at the airport was usually short-lived.

In North Devon, flying operations were initiated at Barnstaple during 1933 when Bob Boyd and Tommy Nash established an airfield alongside the River Taw. Officially opened as the North Devon Airport on 13 June 1934, the Gipsy Moth-equipped Barnstaple and North Devon Flying Club was established, followed by a daily service to Lundy Island, first as Atlantic Coast Air Services and from 26 April 1937 as Lundy and Atlantic Coast Air Services.

On 8 May 1939, Western Airways opened a Manchester to Penzance service calling at Barnstaple, and the same day started a twice-daily Swansea–Barnstaple–Newquay–Penzance service utilizing both Dragon and Dragon Rapide aircraft.

At the outbreak of war, land to the west of the old aerodrome site was requisitioned and work on a new airfield started during May 1940. As RAF Chivenor the new airfield received its first unit during November 1940, in the shape of the Beauforts and Ansons of No. 3 (Coastal) Operational Training Unit (3(C)OTU).

For the next six years Coastal Command reigned supreme at the station, pioneering the new Leigh Light-equipped Wellington GR VIIIs with 172 Squadron. Chivenor was soon to become the home of the Leigh Light Wellingtons that waged a vicious war against the U-boats of Admiral Doenitz. Four squadrons were deployed to Chivenor, and a combination of Air-to-Surface Vessel Mk III radar technology and the breaking of the Enigma code by the cryptographers at Bletchley indicated that intelligence from Ultra could indicate where and when a returning U-boat would surface. The airborne radar could pinpoint the submarine and a Leigh Light-illuminated attack would follow. The Battle of the Atlantic was almost won.

Post-war Chivenor hosted the anti-aircraft cooperation-tasked 691 Squadron, which was renumbered 17 Squadron and joined at the base by the similarly tasked 5 Squadron. The Harvard and Spitfire-equipped 203 Advanced Flying School enjoyed a brief stay at Chivenor until moving to Pembrey on 25 October 1949.

No. 1 Overseas Ferry Unit also briefly stayed at Chivenor, leaving to make space for the Vampire-equipped No. 229 Operational Conversion Unit that during its twenty-three-year stint at the station would in turn fly Sabres and the thoroughbred Hunter, enabling newly trained fast jet pilots to hone their tactical skills.

On 26 April 1935, Provincial Airways opened a new airport at Denbury. Financed and constructed by the airline and frequently referred to as the Torbay Airport, the airfield featured as a scheduled stop on the company's Croydon–Portsmouth–Christchurch–Plymouth route. Railway Air Services also abandoned Haldon for Denbury, nominating the new airfield as a request stop on its weekday Plymouth–Cardiff–Birmingham–Nottingham service.

Provincial Airways ceased operations during September, with Railway Air Services returning to Haldon in time for their 1936 summer service, Denbury having closed with the demise of the former company.

The airport at Exeter was opened to traffic on 31 May 1937 with a major air display taking place on 24 July, as an element of the Devon Air Day that also featured displays at Roborough and Haldon. Royal Air Force participation included the Hornchurch-based Gauntlets of 54 Squadron.

However, the official opening by Sir Kingsley Wood, Secretary of State for Air, would not take place until 30 July 1938, when participation at the opening display included the German aerobatic ace, Herwarth Wendel, flying his swastika-emblazoned Bucker Jungmeister. Whether his visit provided reconnaissance for the later Luftwaffe air raids is unrecorded.

The great air battles fought over Portland during the Battle of Britain period saw the two Exeter-based Hurricane squadrons in the thick of the fighting, alongside the Middle Wallop and Warmwell squadrons. Although now designated RAF Exeter, much of the accommodation was still under canvas.

In November 263 Squadron arrived with their new Westland Whirlwinds and patrolled the Channel to deal with E-boats deployed to collect ditched Luftwaffe aircrew after night raids on west country cities.

During the early months of 1941 the airfield was targeted by the Luftwaffe on five occasions, while on 12 February 1942 a trio of Do 217s bombed the airfield as part of the diversionary tactic to enable the channel dash of the *Scharnhorst* and *Gneisenau*. By April 1942 Exeter had become a sector station and controlled Harrowbeer, Church Stanton and the advanced landing ground at Bolt Head.

For D-Day operations, Exeter was designated as USAAF Station 463. Hosting the four squadrons of the 440th Troop Carrier Group, forty-five C-47s were launched shortly before midnight on 5 June 1944, carrying the American troops of the 101st Airborne Division to the Normandy drop zones (DZ).

Early post-war inhabitants of RAF Exeter were the Meteors of 222 Squadron and the Mosquito NF 30-equipped 151 Squadron. Transferred to Ministry of Civil Aviation control on 1 January 1947, Chrislea Aircraft Ltd moved in from Heston, setting up production of their Super Ace and Sky Jeep aircraft. However, it was contracts obtained for the operation of 10 Reserve Flying School and 3 Civilian Anti-Aircraft Cooperation Unit that ensured a regular income for the airport during the difficult early post-war years.

During 1938, Bertram Arden, a member of a farming family with land on the Exeter bypass, purchased the two-seat Surrey Flying Services AL1 and towed the biplane home by road from Croydon Airport to a field on the bypass, where he flew the aeroplane a great deal until 1939. His initial appetite for flying had been whetted by the pre-war air displays at Hendon.

As the war progressed a number of surplus light aircraft were obtained from the Air Ministry sales at Kemble and after the war they were made airworthy and operated from the bypass, forming the equipment of the Devonshire Flying Club. Operations were suspended in about 1949, and the field is now the head office site of South West Water.

Constructed as a 10 Group fighter station, Harrowbeer was opened on 15 August 1941, as a satellite for Exeter. Situated half a mile west of Yelverton, the station in turn became the home of 302 (Polish) and 312 (Czech) Squadrons, both units flying Spitfires. Operations then centred on fighter-bomber operations with the arrival of the Hurricane-equipped 175 Squadron.

The early months of 1943 saw 263 Squadron move its Whirlwinds to Harrowbeer and operate alongside the Typhoon squadrons that were concentrating their efforts on rail communicatons and airfields in France. As the year drew to a close, 'Noball' operations were flown against the new V-1 sites in France. During the months surrounding D-Day, the station featured in attacks on radar sites, shipping strikes and operations against communications.

Despite Fighter Command closing Harrowbeer on 13 May 1946, 19 Group Communications Flight moved in from Roborough during December 1947 with Ansons and Dominies, remaining until flying activities ended during the late summer of 1948. Ministry of Civil Aviation plans to utilize Harrowbeer as the civil airport for Plymouth foundered in the face of opposition from conservationists, with the site returning to common land.

Constructed to overcome the endurance deficiencies of British day fighters when charged with bomber escort or intruder missions, Bolt Head, situated 1½ miles south-west of Salcombe, was opened in 1941 for 10 and 11 Group fighters when escorting the bombers of 2 Group into western France. Accommodation was sparse with domestic accommodation provided at the Hope Cove GCI station. Early visitors to Bolt Head were Lysanders engaged in providing troops with experience of chemical warfare, and a pair of similar aircraft was operated by 276 Squadron on ASR duties.

The installation of more permanent facilities during 1942 saw the airfield upgraded to satellite status, seeing considerable use by the fighters of the Exeter Wing. A number of units, equipped variously with Typhoons and Spitfires, including Griffon-powered Mk XIIs and the Mk XIVs of 610 Squadron, operated from the clifftop site. Placed on Care and Maintenance on 25 April 1945, the airfield eventually closed during 1947.

Dunkeswell, situated 4 miles north of Honiton and constructed by Wimpey during 1941–2, was allocated for use by 19 Group, Coastal Command, during May 1942. The airfield remained unused until allocated to the United States Navy as the base for Fleet Air Wing 7 which would operate as an element of 19 Group.

Opened for the Americans during July 1943, initial occupants were the temporary anti-submarine squadrons of the USAAF in the shape of the component squadrons of the Liberator-equipped 479th Bombardment Group.

However, only a month was to elapse before the US Navy's VP103 became operational with the PB4Y-1, a specialized anti-submarine version of the Liberator. Dunkeswell then became the UK base for US Navy anti-submarine operations. Further squadrons were eventually assigned to the mid-Devon base with a detachment of PBY-5A Catalinas also operating in the same role. Vacated by the Americans, the immediate post-war years saw the station serving as the home of 3 Overseas Aircraft Preparation Unit, with the RAF eventually relinquishing its interest in February 1949.

Sharing a plateau high in the Blackdown Hills with Dunkeswell, Upottery airfield was completed in time for the D-Day activities of its first occupants, the 439th Troop Carrier Group of the USAAF. Opened at Station 462, the four component squadrons of the 439th were under the command of Colonel Charles H. Young, who led the Group to Normandy in his radar-equipped C-47 during the small hours of 6 June 1944.

Carrying the paratroopers of the 101st Airborne Division, the 81 Douglas C-47 and C-53 Skytrains headed for the DZ near Ste Mère Eglise. The following day gliders were towed to Normandy with re-supply tasks following.

As the fighting in France moved away from the coast, the 439th redeployed to Orbetello airfield, Italy, leaving the runways empty, until runway repairs at Dunkeswell, during November and December 1944, saw the Fleet Air Wing 7 aircraft temporarily flying from Upottery.

On 11 January 1945, 19 Group, Coastal Command, made Upottery available on a full-time basis to the US Navy, which quickly deployed VP107 and VP112 to the new base, taking their part in the submarine war alongside the Dunkeswell units. Vacated when the war in Europe ended, the airfield remained under RAF charge until it was closed during November 1948.

Coastal Command plans for a satellite for Chivenor resulted in the construction of Winkleigh on a stretch of boggy moorland on the outskirts of Winkleigh village. Although work on the site started as early as 1940, the new airfield was not completed until the end of 1942, remaining unoccupied by flying units until the airfield was utilized for USAAF operations in connection with American troops rehearsing invasion exercises on North Devon's Atlantic beaches.

However, it was the four-month period starting in April 1944 that saw the main operational use of the airfield. Moving from Exeter, 406 (RCAF) Squadron almost immediately started to re-equip with Mosquito night-fighters, in place of the unit's Beaufighters. Operating the squadron's first operational night sortie in the Mosquito, during the night of 29/30 April, Squadron Leader 'Blackie' Williams and Flying Officer 'Kirk' Kirkpatrick downed a pair of Do 217s in the space of eleven minutes. Williams was later appointed commanding officer of the unit, which remained at Winkleigh until moving to Colerne on 16 September.

The same summer saw elements of 286 Squadron operating Hurricanes and Defiants, while 415 (RCAF) Squadron operated a detachment of Albacores to deter E-boats from penetrating the allied training and marshalling area prior to D-Day. During July, Lysander aircraft of 161 Squadron deployed to Winkleigh, tasked with delivering and collecting SOE personnel operating in western France.

Winkleigh's last occupants were the Norwegian Air Force, who operated the station as a training base in preparation for the rebirth of the Royal Norwegian Air Force. Twenty-two Harvard and twenty-two Cornell aircraft were operated over a ten-month period, until November 1945 when flying at Winkleigh ceased, and the Norwegian aircraft moved to their new base at Gardermoen, near Oslo.

Today Exeter and Plymouth ply their trade as civil airports while Dunkeswell plays host to private flyers, who prefer the club-like social atmosphere of an airfield that fifty years ago waged a long and dangerous war against the U-boats, while Devon's sole remaining military airfield at Chivenor is again poised to close in the face of defence cuts.

Elsewhere the wind blows across decaying runways and through the broken windows of long-forgotten Nissen huts, while if ghosts could speak, those at Upottery and Winkleigh would have distinct North American accents!

Keith A. Saunders, 1994

Acknowledgements

This work would not have been possible without the assistance of all those who provided photographs and information. Special mention must also be made of the darkroom skills of John Wilson and Rex Hitchcock.

D. Acland • D. Arden • P. Arnold

R.P. Beamont CBE, DSO, DFC, DL, FRAeS • D. Benfield • P.W. Berridge

the late G.W. Causey • B. Chapman • J. Chapman • N.C. Collier

R.D. Cox • H. Crawford, Devon Library Services • K. Gourd • J. Gregory

D. Green • R.J. Herman • B.R. Holt • R.T. Jackson • the late W.K. Kilsby

Wg. Cdr. E.H. King OBE, RAF (Ret'd) • R.L. Knight Ltd • E. Loosemoore

L.W. Lownds-Pateman MBE • R. Manley • J.G. Munro • D. Newcombe

A.P. Paddon • R.J. Parkhouse • M.W. Payne • the late G. Raby • L. Retallick

R.T. Riding • the late G. Taylor • Flt. Lt. A.S. Thomas RAF

Tiverton Museum • Mrs T. Tutt • US National Archives • D. Vosper

SECTION ONE

Barnstaple (North Devon Aerodrome)

On two occasions in 1933 and on 1 August 1934, Alan Cobham's National Aviation Day Ltd visited the airfield. The Handley Page HP 33 Clive I G-ABYX carried 20,000 passengers on joy rides with Cobham before being scrapped in 1935.

Blackburn Lincock II G-AALH provided aerobatic displays with National Aviation Day Ltd at Barnstaple.

Female admirers look on as the pilot of the de Havilland DH82 Tiger Moth tinkers with the 120 hp Gipsy III engine while the Blackburn Lincock taxis for take-off.

High over North Devon is de Havilland DH82 Tiger Moth G-ABUL, with the occupant of the front cockpit out on the wing talking to the occupant of the rear cockpit.

Aerial view of the Blackburn Lincock and Handley Page HP33 Clive I parked on the airfield.

The crowd look on as passengers wait to board the de Havilland DH83 Fox Moth G-ACEY (nearest to the camera), with the Handley Page HP33 in the background.

Cierva C19 Mk IV G-ABFZ toured with the National Aviation Day fleet and made demonstration flights at Barnstaple.

The National Aviation Day display returned to Barnstaple in 1934. The Mongoose-powered Avro 504N is shown providing joy rides on 1 August.

Lundy and Atlantic Coast Airlines operated Short S16 Scion 1 G-ACUW on *ad hoc* charters and on the daily Barnstaple–Lundy Island service. The company had previously traded as Atlantic Coast Air Services.

Members of the Barnstaple and North Devon Flying Club, with Lundy and Atlantic Coast Airline's de Havilland DH60 Gipsy Moth G-AAIM in the background.

On 8 May 1939 the Straight Corporation-owned Western Airways inaugurated a daily Swansea–Barnstaple–Newquay–Penzance service. Their DH84 Dragon G-ACMJ is pictured at Barnstaple.

Resting at Barnstaple while operating on the Swansea–Penzance service of Western Airways, Dragon Rapide G-ADDD was previously on the strength of the King's Flight.

RAF Bolt Head

275 Squadron operated Walrus Is on search and rescue duties from Bolt Head between August and October 1944 and again between October 1944 and February 1945. Flight Lieutenant D.F.R. Emms AFC, a Flight Commander, is seen with a squadron Walrus and colleagues from the squadron.

Although 276 Squadron operated from Harrowbeer in the ASR role, the crew of this Lysander III is believed to have been pictured at Bolt Head during early 1942.

RAF Chivenor

During 1940 the site of the North Devon Aerodrome was extended and became RAF Chivenor. Coastal Command crews received operational training with 3(C)OTU and 5 (C)OTU. The first unit to arrive in November was 3(C)OTU; the equipment of both units included Beauforts.

Members of 172 Squadron, with Heanton Parish Church as the backdrop. The Chivenor-based squadron was the first unit to operate the Leigh Light-equipped Wellington.

Snow is cleared from the wings of a 14 Squadron Wellington.

14 Squadron operated in the anti-submarine role from Chivenor with Leigh Light-equipped Wellington GRXIV aircraft. This disastrous fire appears to have occurred after the aircraft collided with high ground.

Post-war study of a Mosquito VI from 248 Squadron, seen over Bideford Bay before the squadron moved to Thorney Island on 31 May 1946.

Based at Chivenor for anti-aircraft cooperation duties, 691 Squadron was renumbered 17 Squadron on 11 February 1949. This Beaufighter TT10 was operated by the squadron.

17 Squadron Spitfire LF16E SL549.

Airspeed Oxford of 17 Squadron.

Spitfire LF16E TE406 of 203 Advanced Flying School crashed on Dartmoor on 23 October 1947. Its remains were still to be seen on the moor in 1964 when this picture of the tail-fin was taken.

1 Overseas Ferry Unit was present at Chivenor from July 1950 until March 1951, with a mixed bag of types that included Buckmaster 1 RP232.

229 Operational Conversion Unit (OCU) arrived at Chivenor on 28 March 1951. Initial equipment was the DH Vampire FB5, two examples of which are pictured on the Chivenor flight line.

229 OCU DH Vampire FB5 VV480 suffered engine failure over the Bristol Channel. The pilot, Flt Lt Bill Wood, made a forced landing on the beach at Woolacombe. Kept above the incoming tide, the Vampire flew again some seven months later.

The RAF's last Lancasters were operated by the School of Maritime Reconnaissance at St Mawgan until withdrawn in October 1956. RF326 is seen here in the static display at Chivenor on Battle of Britain Day, 15 September 1956.

During April 1955 Chivenor received the graceful Hawker Hunter F1. Later versions of the Hunter remained in service with 229 OCU until the station closed in 1973.

During 1957 229 OCU received the improved Hunter F4. These eight examples carry the nose markings of 234 (Reserve) Squadron.

Hunter F4 XF938 pictured during its landing run at Chivenor.

During 1958, the Chivenor OCU became the first unit to receive the new two-seat Hunter T7. XL586 was an early example.

Mosquito TT35 from 3 CAACU at Exeter lends variety to the static park during the 1959 Battle of Britain Air Display.

The Anson T21 WD415 of Station Flight forms part of the static park for the Battle of Britain Air Display, September 1960.

The Supermarine Swift, the first British swept-wing fighter to enter service with the Royal Air Force, encountered control problems and was quickly withdrawn from service. The developed Swift FR5 was employed in the fighter reconnaissance role, with this Jever-based example from 2 Squadron making a rare UK appearance for Chivenor's Royal Observer Corps Day, 4 October 1959.

Denbury
(Torbay Airport)

Denbury Airport, serving Newton Abbot, Teignmouth and Torquay, only existed for a short time. An army of labourers was employed in land drainage before the opening of the airport on 26 April 1935. Note the lack of sophisticated plant equipment available to the construction force.

Denbury was included only in the 1935 schedules of Railway Air Services and Provincial Airways, with the latter's DH Dragon G-ACDL seen on the opening day. The airfield is now the site of HM Prison Channings Wood.

An unidentified Miles Hawk Major about to start its take-off run from Denbury on 26 April 1935. The aerodrome was prepared for and operated by Provincial Airways.

Pictured by an amateur photographer on 26 April 1935, the landing aircraft is probably the Miles M3A Falcon Major G-ADHG.

Looking over the hedge, the Miles Falcon Major taxis for take-off, followed by the Dragon of Provincial Airways.

SECTION FIVE
Dunkeswell

A PB4Y-1 Liberator of Fleet Air Wing 7 catches the setting sun as it passes the Dunkeswell tower. The US Navy based both PB4Y-1 Liberators and PBY-5A Catalinas at the Devon base from the summer of 1943 until the end of the Second World War.

Up from Dunkeswell, a PB4Y-1 Liberator of Fleet Air Wing 7 pictured over Coleford village. On the night of 12 November 1943 this aircraft, under the command of Lt. R.B. Brownell, sank U-508 but was itself shot down by return fire from the submarine. The Liberator crew received posthumous awards.

About to begin another lengthy sea search, an Erco-turreted PB4Y-1 Liberator taxis for take-off at Dunkeswell.

Ground crew prepare a PB4Y-1. The nose inscription reads 'TALLY HO/THE FOX/SHE RUNS!'

Seafire IICs, MA996 nearest camera, at Dunkeswell on 6 September 1944, while attached to Fleet Air Wing 7 for fighter affiliation.

B-17s from Polebrook's 351st Bombardment Group (BG) parked on the Dunkeswell runway after a diversionary landing during December 1944. Clark Gable flew missions with the 351st BG.

351st B-17s above Dunkeswell.

A Fleet Air Wing 7 aircraft in a Dunkeswell hangar for a routine 120-hour check, 29 November 1943.

Exeter Airport

Two Scions from Plymouth over the Devon countryside during the opening to traffic of
Exeter Airport, 31 May 1937.

A quartet of Hornchurch-based Gauntlet IIs of 54 Squadron at Exeter Airport for Devon Air Day, 24 July 1937. During the day the team also displayed at Roborough and Haldon.

Exeter Airport was officially opened by Sir Kingsley Wood, Secretary of State for Air, on Saturday 30 July 1938. Aerobatics were provided by 151 Squadron with Gauntlets from North Weald.

Precision aerobatics for the opening display were also provided by German aerobatic ace, Herwarth Wendel, in a Bucker Jungmeister.

Wolfgang Vogt attends to the engine of the German Jungmeister, while an unidentified official looks on.

Miles Hawk Trainer G-AFEW visiting Exeter during 1938 from the Straight Corporation-owned Plymouth Flying Club.

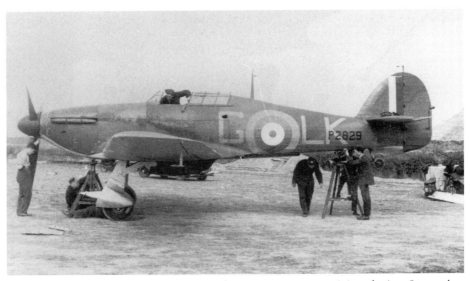

Hurricane I P2829 of 87 Squadron undergoes open-air servicing during September 1940.

During the Battle of Britain, the Hurricane-equipped 87 and 213 Squadrons were deployed to Exeter to protect the channel ports and Portland Naval Base from air attack. Apart from London and Liverpool, Portland was scheduled for more main formation raids than any other target during the Battle of Britain. Flying Officer 'Watty' Watson of 87 Squadron with Hurricane P2829 is pictured.

At Exeter during the summer of 1940, the nineteen-year-old Pilot Officer 'Bee' Beamont, fought with 87 Squadron, destroying two Luftwaffe aircraft, in the bloody air battles over Portland. Retiring with the rank of Wing Commander, he holds a CBE, DSO and Bar, DFC and Bar and an American DFC.

'Bee' Beamont and Hurricane at Exeter, summer 1940.

Flying Officer W.D. David with 87 Squadron
at Exeter during the Battle of Britain, when
his score climbed to twenty. Retiring with the
rank of Wing Commander, his decorations
and awards include a CBE, DFC and Bar and
an AFC.

Pilot Officer A.C.R. McLure downed a Messerschmitt Bf 109 near Portland on 11 August 1940. Return fire caused him to make a wheels-up landing near Warmwell at 11.10 a.m.

Flight Sergeant 'Chiefy' Matthews of 'A' Flight, 87 Squadron, summer 1940.

Sergeant Thoroughgood, a sergeant pilot, with 'A' Flight, 87 Squadron.

A detached flight was operated by 87 Squadron at Bibury. Pictured there in early August 1940 are, left to right: 'Watty' Watson, 'Harry' Tait, 'Widge' Gleed, 'Roddy' Rayner and 'Peter' Comely. Peter was shot down and killed over Portland on 15 August.

The Hurricane-equipped 504 (County of Nottingham) Squadron was stationed at Exeter from 26 September 1940 until July of the following year. Hurricane V6732 is seen here after a collision with an airfield contractor's car.

Hindered from achieving maximum potential by Peregrine engines that failed to develop full rated power at altitude, the Westland Whirlwind was held back from the Battle of Britain and first flew operationally with 263 Squadron at Exeter on 7 December 1940, despite having taken part in fighter affiliation exercises with 21 Squadron at Lossiemouth on 15 September 1940.

Sqn. Ldr. J.G. Munro, the Commanding Officer of 263 Squadron at Exeter, December 1940.

Flt. Lt. T.P. Pugh with a Whirlwind at Exeter during January 1941.

January 1941 and a 263 Squadron Whirlwind taxis for take-off at Exeter.

Spitfire IX MH852 of 131 Squadron.

Pilots of the Spitfire V-equipped 131 Squadron stroll for the camera during the summer of 1943.

On 18 April 1944 USAAF's 440th Troop Carrier Group (TCG) deployed to Exeter in readiness for 6 June and 'Overlord'. C-47s of the 440th TCG are pictured at Exeter during the evening of 5 June, prior to carrying American paratroopers to Normandy later the same night.

The Exeter-built Chrislea CH3 Series 2 Super Ace G-AKFD prepares for an air-to-air photo session with Bertram Arden's Auster 5 G-AJHJ in 1948. Much of wartime RAF Exeter forms the background.

The brand new Super Ace G-AKFD high above the Devon countryside. The Chrislea Aircraft Co. Ltd constructed both Super Aces and Skyjeeps at Exeter between 1947 and 1952.

Bertram Arden's Taylorcraft Plus C G-AFTN visiting Exeter from his private airfield on the Exeter bypass.

Bertram Arden's Auster 5 G-AJHJ visits Exeter Airport.

Tiger Moth R5243 of 10 Reserve Flying School that was formed at Exeter on 16 May 1949. It later operated Chipmunks until it was disbanded on 19 April 1954.

After the war and at some time before September 1949, Miles Hawk Trainer G-AHUK is towed into a hangar by the airport ambulance.

In March 1951, airport authorities were contracted to operate 3 Civilian Anti-Aircraft Cooperation Unit (3 CAACU). Spitfire 21 LA322 formed part of the early equipment of the unit.

Spitfire 16 TE456 of 3 CAACU, pictured here in 1956, starred in the film *Reach for the Sky*, the story of Douglas Bader, and is now exhibited in the Auckland War Memorial Museum.

Bristol Beaufighter TT10s towed targets for 3 CAACU. Here RD854 is seen landing at Exeter, *c.* 1953.

Mosquito TT35s replaced the Beaufighter in the target towing role. The aircraft illustrated, TH998, when withdrawn from service was presented to the Smithsonian Institution in Washington DC.

Mosquito TT35 TA634 of 3 CAACU.

The mid-1950s saw Vampire FB5s join 3 CAACU. Here VZ304 is illustrated.

Another example of a 3 CAACU Vampire FB5 WE840.

Vampire T11s eventually replaced the single seat FB5s at Exeter. Later XH304 joined the 'Vintage Pair' until destroyed in a fatal mid-air collision with the Meteor operated by the team.

Boulton Paul Balliol T2s of 3 CAACU at Exeter Air Day, 28 June 1958.

Pictured at Exeter Air Day, the massive bulk of Gloster Javelin FAW2 XA802 from 46 Squadron at Odiham, 28 June 1958.

During 1960 a handful of Hawker Hunter F4s were operated by 3 CAACU. WV401 is pictured at Exeter Air Day, 9 July 1960.

Tiger Moth G-AHWE was operated by the Exeter Aero Club during the 1950s.

Tiger Moth G-AIDD of the Plymouth and District Aero Club parked at Exeter during the mid-1950s.

Auster Autocrat G-AJIP was operated by the Exeter Aero Club.

Airport Manager W.R. Parkhouse flew his Hornet Moth G-AESE to Vienna during May 1956, to collect a Paul Tissandier Diploma, awarded by the Fédération Aéronautique Internationale, for services to civil aviation.

The Fairchild Argus was built in quantity for USAAF communications during the Second World War. This civil registered example, seen hangared at Exeter in 1955, had previously been supplied to the RAF under Lend-Lease.

The bright red Auster 5 G-AJXC, visiting Exeter from its base at Chivenor during the late 1950s.

Pictured on an *ad hoc* charter to Exeter on 3 September 1959, Viking 1 G-AGRW is in the colours of Hunting Clan.

Jersey Airlines operated their first regular scheduled service on 7 April 1952, pioneering the post-war Exeter–Jersey sector. Rapide G-AKNE was the second aircraft acquired by the airline.

During 1954 Jersey Airlines received the first of six DH Heron fourteen to seventeen seat airliners. This was the first Jersey aircraft to carry a hostess! G-ANWZ awaits its passengers at Exeter, 26 July 1957.

During the summer of 1959, Starways called at Exeter on their Liverpool–Newquay sector. Here DC-4 G-APEZ loads passengers with its four mighty 1,540 hp Pratt & Whitney Twin Wasps at idle.

Dakota IV G-AMPO of Starways taxis at Exeter for departure to Newquay, 27 June 1959.

Exeter Bypass

Bertram Arden first operated from the old Heles School playing field on the Exeter bypass when he acquired the Surrey Flying Services AL1 on 20 May 1938. The two-seat, single-engine biplane was built by Surrey Flying Services at Croydon during 1929.

Bertram Arden with the Surrey AL1, *c.* 1938.

A rustic setting, as the Cirrus engine of BA Swallow G-AFHC receives attention.

Five BA Swallows were acquired and three were operated post-war from the Exeter bypass including the Pobjoy-engined G-AFGC.

A group of would-be aviators with BA Swallow G-AFGC.

During later operations a field, now occupied by the head office of South West Water, replaced the earlier field and a purpose-built hangar was erected. A single seat Mercedes-Benz poses with the Auster 5 G-AJHJ.

Auster 5 G-AJHJ after an incident with a boundary hedge.

The Devonshire Flying Club was formed during the late 1940s. Here the Auster 5 is refuelled from a can.

The Tiger Moth G-ACDA/BB724 is towed on to the bypass by an upright Ford saloon.

The Auster 5 is pictured alongside the hangar with hay-making in progress.

Haldon

In April 1928, Avro 594 Avian III G-EBXO was purchased from the manufacturers by Haldon Aerodrome owner William Parkhouse. Witney Straight, later to become a director of BOAC, learned to fly at Haldon in the aeroplane, which he purchased during the summer of 1928 from the aerodrome owner.

William Parkhouse landed on the golf course at Haldon, 6 May 1928. He was flying this Avian, which was towed down the hill into Teignmouth and placed on display in the Bank Street showrooms of the Agra Engineering Company which he owned. Many years later Lady Daphne Straight was heard to reminisce that Teignmouth had been the only town in England with an aeroplane shop!

The showrooms of the Agra Engineering Company in Bank Street, Teignmouth. The premises are now occupied by Woolworths.

W.R. Parkhouse and the Chief Constable of the Devon Constabulary, Major L.H. Morris (centre), discuss the aerial hunt for escaped Dartmoor prisoners with PC59 of the Devon Constabulary.

An early example of the autogiro, Cierva C19 Mk1 G-AAGL, is pictured at Haldon after a landing accident, during the first Haldon flying meeting, 21 September 1929.

The visiting aircraft park at Haldon for the flying meeting on 21 September 1929. In the foreground is coupé Moth G-AADX, one of eight special enclosed examples fitted with Triplex glazing.

Sir Sefton Brancker, the Director of Civil Aviation, attended the 1929 meeting in his specially marked Cirrus II Moth G-EDCA. He was later to lose his life in the R101 disaster at Beauvais on 5 October 1930.

An early picture of DH60G Gipsy Moth G-AAJG. William Parkhouse operated a sales agency for de Havilland aircraft, illustrated by the £595 sales tag on the rudder.

The Cirrus III-powered Westland IV prototype G-EBXK visited Haldon during 1929.

Junkers F13 G-AAGU operated from Croydon Airport and is shown during a visit to Haldon. Later sold to South African Airways, it crashed on 29 January 1936.

The Honourable Richard Westernra with his Gipsy Moth G-ABJL in the grounds of Luscombe Castle at Dawlish, March 1932.

Richard Westernra and his wife lived at Bishopsteignton and both were enthusiastic sporting pilots during the 1930s. Pictured at Haldon, where they hangared their aircraft, is the single-seat DH60GIII Moth G-ACCW, outright winner of the 1933 London to Newcastle Air Race at 125.25 mph, with the Honourable Richard at the controls. The Haldon clubhouse is behind the Moth.

The Honourable Mrs Richard Westernra set out from Croydon to fly to the Cape on 6 November 1931. The return journey was made in seventy-two days. The DH80A Puss Moth G-ABJO used for the flight is pictured at Sywell, on Whit Monday, 5 June 1933, when it was being used by the Westernras to attend the Sywell Annual Air Pageant.

On 12 April 1933 the GWR Air Service inaugurated a twice-daily weekday service between Cardiff and Plymouth (Roborough), via Haldon. The aircraft used was the Westland Wessex G-AAGW, chartered from Imperial Airways and painted in GWR's colours of cream and brown. The service was later extended to Birmingham (Castle Bromwich).

This aerial view of Haldon was taken during 1933 when the touring air circus, British Hospitals' Air Pageant, visited on its national fund-raising tour for UK hospitals.

Spartan 1 three-seater G-ABYN provided joy rides with British Hospitals' Air Pageant at Haldon. The elderly biplane is currently being restored to flying condition at Southampton after over half a century in storage at a sawmill in Eire.

Programme cover from the British Hospitals' Air Pageant visit to Haldon.

HRH The Prince of Wales talks with William Parkhouse and his wife Vera at Haldon, 28 May 1930. The Prince lunched at Haldon while visiting Torquay and the RAF airfield at Folley Gate, near Okehampton. The Prince's Gipsy Moth stands behind the group.

The 1935 King's Cup-winning Miles M3B Falcon Six G-ADLC at Haldon, 26 April 1936. 'Dougie' Gourd, a Bishopsteignton bus and coach operator, poses for the occasion.

During 1934 Provincial Airways included Haldon as a stop on their Plymouth–
Southampton–Croydon service. DH Dragon G-ACKD *Saturn* prepares to taxi for the
grass runway.

William Parkhouse overflies the Haldon hangar and a row of parked aircraft in his Gipsy Moth.

Trials of landing aids were undertaken at Haldon with the Fairey IIIF IIIM S1399.

Probably one of the largest aeroplanes to land at Haldon, the Vickers Virginia is believed to have featured in the trials of landing aids.

The last aircraft to land regularly at Haldon, spring 1968. Piper Tri-Pacer 160 G-ARFD was flown to Haldon by a member of the landowner's family, when on weekend leave from the Army.

The disused airfield at Haldon passes below the author, 8 June 1968.

The Haldon clubhouse in derelict condition during 1977, shortly before its demise by fire at the hands of inebriated Hell's Angels.

RAF Harrowbeer

For two months during October and November 1941, 130 Squadron operated Spitfire VBs out of Harrowbeer on shipping patrols, sweeps and bomber escorts before moving to Warmwell. AD370 PJ-C is illustrated.

276 Squadron operated from Harrowbeer in the air-sea rescue role from October 1941 until 3 April 1944. Typical equipment was the Spitfire IIA. Detachments were deployed at Warmwell, Perranporth, Fairwood Common and Portreath.

Hurricane IIB HV555 'HH-E' of 175 Squadron at Harrowbeer, October 1942. Two months later the squadron moved to Gatwick.

Typhoon IB EJ967 'DP-D' of 193 Squadron at Harrowbeer, 3 September 1943. The unit was operating sweeps, escorts and anti-'Rhubarb' patrols, attempting to catch the Bf 109G and FW 190 fighter-bombers that were raiding coastal towns.

Squadron Leader J.J. O'Meara DSO DFC of 131 Squadron coming to grips with airfield defences at Harrowbeer.

Pictured in a 131 Squadron Spitfire VII, Ted King retired with the rank of Wing Commander, and later became a post-war CFI with the Exeter Flying Club.

Based at Harrowbeer for search and rescue duties, 275 Squadron was commanded by Squadron Leader Eric Seabourne DFC, who is pictured with a Spitfire VB from the unit during June 1944.

Spitfire IXs were operated from Harrowbeer by 64 Squadron during July and August 1944 in the anti-'Rhubarb' and bomber escort roles.

Based at Harrowbeer between July and August 1944, 126 Squadron operated its Spitfire IXs in support of the advancing Allied troops in France. MK126 5J-G is illustrated.

A general view of Harrowbeer with a pair of Mustang Is of 26 Squadron in the foreground, summer 1945.

SECTION TEN
RAF Mount Batten

Mount Batten was initially known as RNAS Cattewater and operated as a First World War seaplane base. The US Navy's NC-4 flying boat reached Plymouth, having completed the first aerial crossing of the Atlantic, on 31 May 1919.

A trio of Southampton Is of 204 Squadron at Mount Batten.

204 Squadron re-equipped with Saro London Is during October 1936 and retained the type until replaced by Sunderlands during the summer of 1939.

From December 1937 to May 1938, five Londons of 204 Squadron carried out a cruise of 30,000 miles from England to New South Wales and back. Special long-range fuel tanks were fitted above the hull. London K6927 is pictured departing from Mount Batten for Australia on 2 December 1937.

Sunderland I L5802 of 204 Squadron, summer 1939.

The station will for ever be synonymous with the Short Sunderland and the activities of 10 (Royal Australian Air Force) Squadron against the U-boat menace. A Sunderland of 10 Squadron is pictured in Plymouth Sound.

Sunderland I W3984 of 10 Squadron.

HRH The Duke of Kent inspecting 10 Squadron personnel at Mount Batten.

Roborough Airport – Plymouth

Pictured at Roborough with his Percival Mew Gull G-AEXF, Alex Henshaw, trail blazer and wartime Spitfire test pilot, was about to compete in the Devon Air Race, 24 July 1937. Held over a triangular course, with turning points at Haldon and Exeter airports, Henshaw finished in sixth place at an average of 208 mph.

Captain Percival Phillips of Air Publicity surprised the handicappers, averaging 103 mph and claiming victory in the 1937 Devon Air Race in his Avro 504N G-ADEV.

C.G.M. Allington in the tiny Dart Kitten G-AEXT waits for the starter in the 1937 Devon Air Race.

Runner-up to Captain Phillips was Miss Constance Leathart who averaged 120 mph in the Comper Swift G-ABUU.

Short S16 Scion 2 G-ADDX, was operated pre-war by Plymouth Airport Ltd on *ad hoc* charters, and carried the striped rudder of the Straight Corporation, the airfield operators.

Summer 1935 and the de Havilland Fox Moth G-ACEX of Provincial Airways waits to depart from Roborough for Croydon via Denbury and Southampton.

De Havilland Dragon G-ADDI *City of Cardiff* of Railway Air Services is prepared for its return journey to Nottingham via Denbury, Cardiff and Birmingham, summer 1935.

247 Squadron stationed a flight of Gloster Gladiators at Roborough during 1940. The only biplane fighters to remain in front-line RAF service during the Battle of Britain, the aircraft illustrated, N2306, was flown by Sgt. Derek Lawford.

On 14 June 1941, 'C' Flight of 2 Anti-Aircraft Cooperation Unit (2 AACU) moved to Roborough from Cleave. Messing facilities for groundcrew were sparse!

A Nissen hut on the airfield provided accommodation for airmen, with heating provided by the coke-burning stove in the centre of the picture.

A Bedford truck provides a prop for this picture of 2 AACU groundcrew.

Gladiator II N2308 was operated by 2 AACU when tasked with gun-laying exercises.

Hector I K9783 of 2 AACU after an accident at Roborough, 27 February 1942.

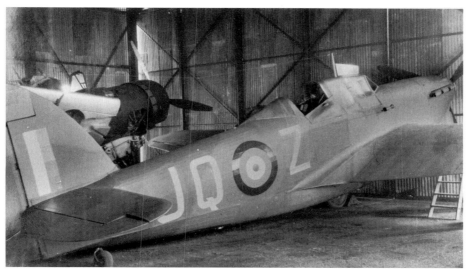

Hawker Henleys were operated by 2 AACU for target towing duties, with this example photographed in the hangar at Roborough.

'C' Flight of 2 AACU became 1623 (AAC) Flight on 14 February 1943. Equipment included Airspeed Oxford N6275.

Hurricane P2865 of 286 Squadron was 'acquired' by 1623 (AAC) Flight, after a landing accident at Roborough.

Miles Gemini 1A G-AKHW *City of Plymouth* was a veteran of a decade in club and taxi service at Roborough and retained the livery of British Overseas Airways Corporation, the original owners.

Miles Messenger 2A G-AKBM joined the Plymouth & District Aero Club in 1948 and remained at the airport until withdrawn from use in 1961, when it was dismantled at Weston-super-Mare.

The Tiger Moth-equipped Britannia Royal Naval College Air Experience Flight was formed at Roborough during the late 1950s. Maintenance was contracted to Airwork. The aeroplane illustrated was built during the war as T6099, civilianized as G-AOGR and re-mustered as XL714 in August 1956.

SECTION TWELVE

Upottery

The airfield was opened on 17 February 1944 and became USAAF Station 462. In preparation for D-Day, Col Charles H. Young's 439th Troop Carrier Group (TCG) with its component 91st, 92nd, 93rd and 94th Troop Carrier Squadrons deployed to Upottery. The picture shows *The Argonia*, C-47A No. 43-15159 (D8-Z) on its return to the airfield from Normandy on 6 June 1944. Note the flak damage to the port wing. The airfield was eventually closed during November 1948.

In the cabin of *The Argonia*, C-47A No. 43-15159 (D8-Z), 439th TCG, 29 May 1944, just before take-off on the last practice mission before D-Day, leading a formation of eighty-one aircraft from Upottery. Left to right: S/Sgt. John A. Dougherty, Radio Operator, 1st Lt. Adam Parsons, Co-pilot, 2nd Lt. Vincent J. Paterno, Navigator, Lt. Col. Charles H. Young, Pilot (Group CO).

Loading members of the 506th Parachute Infantry Regiment, 101st Airborne Division, at Upottery on the late evening of 5 June 1944. The pilot, 2nd Lt. Martin N. Neill, is standing at the left edge of the photo; his C-47 was No. 42-93004 (D8-T), 94th Troop Carrier Squadron of the 439th TCG. Lt. Carl George is in the doorway helping paratroopers aboard. The big hunched-over trooper is unknown, while the stocky trooper is probably Bill McNeese. Jacobs is beyond the big trooper.

Upottery with troops preparing to load, 7 June 1944. These gliders were part of a formation of thirty Horsas and twenty Waco CG-4A gliders towed from Upottery to near Ste Mère Eglise, France, by the 439th TCG. The 82nd Airborne Division troops carried by the 439th were members of the 2nd Bn, 325th Glider Infantry, or of the 2nd Bn., 401st Glider Infantry, which was attached to the 325th and acted as its third battalion.

RAF Winkleigh

A Canadian airman poses at Winkleigh with a Beaufighter VIf of 406 (RCAF) Squadron, summer 1944.

Squadron Leader 'Blackie' Williams and Flying Officer 'Kirk' Kirkpatrick with their Mosquito XII at Winkleigh, 4 May 1944. On the night of 29 April 1944, the pair had downed two Dornier Do 217s in only eleven minutes. Williams was appointed CO of the squadron during July.

The aircrew of 406 (RCAF) Squadron.

An anonymous groundcrew member pictured with a Mosquito XXX.

During July 1944, 406 (RCAF) Squadron was re-equipped with the improved Mosquito XXX. A group of Canadian airmen is seen here with MUSH JUNIOR, 30 August 1944.

Countywide

Dawlish, 1923, and de Havilland's Chief Test Pilot, Hubert Broad, collects company chairman, Alan Butler, from Luscombe Castle, where he had been visiting Sir Peter Hoare. The aircraft is DH9C G-EBCZ.

Miles M3A Falcon Major G-AETN pictured after its crash at Duckaller, Dawlish, 17 May 1937. The pilot was killed and two passengers injured.

Langdon Hospital, Dawlish, 27 January 1943. *Werewolf*, a B-17F Flying Fortress that landed on a single engine after being damaged by Luftwaffe fighters during a raid on the French coast submarine pens, arrives unexpectedly.

Lt. George J. Oxrider, the pilot of *Werewolf*, had ordered his crew to bale out of the crippled bomber as the Fortress crossed the Devon coast.

All four engines of the Fortress required changing at Langdon. Oxrider and his crew were from the 358th Bombardment Squadron of the 303rd Bombardment Group, USAAF, based at Molesworth, Huntingdonshire.

US engineers cleared trees, walls and hedges to make a 2,250-ft runway to enable the repaired *Werewolf* to be flown out of Langdon.

Devonport, 1959. The sad remains of the prototype DH Sea Hornet PR22 rest in a Civil Defence training area. The aeroplane had previously been used in a fire-fighting demonstration at a Plymouth air display.

Arena Park, Whipton, Exeter. This was a compulsory stop on the 1911 Circuit of Britain air race. Here Lt. Jean Conneau of the French Navy talks with officials shortly after his arrival in a Bleriot. He averaged 45 mph over the 1,010-mile circuit.

Arena Park, Exeter. Jules Vedrines, the eventual runner-up, discusses his progress with officials shortly after landing in his Morane-Borel.

Arena Park, Exeter. The Deperdussin of James Valentine is waiting at the control. Valentine finished the race in third position.

Arena Park, Exeter. S.F. Cody prepares to leave, 27 July 1911. Flying his Cody Circuit of Britain biplane known as the 'Cathedral', he finished fourth, in the only British aircraft to finish the course.

A lady of the 1920s contemplates her first flight in an Avro 504K of the Cornwall Aviation Co. Ltd from a field near the Gallows, Exeter.

Northernhay Gardens, Exeter, and a captured Messerschmitt Bf 109E is exhibited during September 1940 to raise money for the city's Spitfire fund. Organized by F.D. Beasley of Alphington, the Messerschmitt had force-landed at Faversham, Kent, on 30 August 1940, and was delivered without notice to Mr Beasley's home on a Sunday morning.

Curious villagers examine Short S16 Scion I G-ACUZ at Kingsteignton. Pictured after a forced landing at Whiteway Barton in 1935, the aeroplane was operated by Airwork Ltd at Tollerton.

Exeter Speedway riders, Gordon Taylor (centre) and Bernard 'Bronco' Slade (right) pose at Kennford with the Mignet Pou de Ciel (Flying Flea) G-AEBA that had been purchased by Taylor in Cornwall.

Operating the Flying Flea from a farm field at Kennford continued after the Second World War ban on civil flying. The Pou is seen after a minor landing mishap.

During 1942 the Western Garage, Newton Abbot, closed its doors to the public and began to repair and service aircraft parts, mainly wing and fuselage sections from Beaufighter and Spitfire aircraft. Illustrated are Spitfire wings under repair.

Wings and fuselages were dispersed to the Western Garage and other facilities in the locality from contractors at Exeter. Here a fuselage section receives attention at the Western Garage.

The largely female workforce at the Western Garage was typical of industry during the Second World War.

Folley Gate Airfield, Okehampton, was occasionally used for army cooperation flying between 1928 and the 1950s. It is unclear whether this 16 Squadron Lysander was photographed at Folley Gate or Weston Zoyland.

In April 1914 the Avro 504 prototype had been purchased by the *Daily Mail* and toured the country giving pleasure flights. Fitted with an interchangeable twin float undercarriage, its first flights as a seaplane were made at Paignton.

Avro Anson I K6182 after a forced landing on the Green at Paignton, 4 January 1940. It was operated by 48 Squadron at Thorney Island.

The racecourse at Saltram Park, Plymouth, was initially used as an airship base during the First World War. Subsequent use included joy riding by the Berkshire Aviation Co. with Avro 504K G-EAKX.

The polo ground at Roborough, Plymouth, was utilized by Surrey Flying Services during 1925 for joy riding. This is Avro 504K G-EBHM.

The polo ground operation by Surrey Flying Services included Avro 536 G-EAKM.

Star of the Agricultural Show held at South Molton in July 1911 was a Bleriot XI flown by a Captain Clayton. During the first demonstration flight the engine failed and the forced landing saw the Bleriot damaged, fortunately without injury.

The first DH82A Tiger Moth G-ACDA of the pre-war Hatfield-based de Havilland School of Flying is stored in its wartime impressment colours as BB724. This 1959 photograph was taken at Thorns Cross, Haldon.

Thorns Cross: Auster 5 G-AJHJ shares a barn in 1959 with an elderly bus and a Tiger Moth (right) that hides in the shadows.

Henri Salmet talks with officials after landing at Knightshayes, Tiverton, during his *Daily Mail*-sponsored tour of Devon and Cornwall, June 1912.

Spectators at Knightshayes await their first opportunity to see an aeroplane fly, June 1912.

The former Imperial Airways Handley Page HP42W G-AAXD *Horatius* was wrecked in a forced landing on Tiverton golf course, 7 November 1939. It had been operating trooping and cargo services for the British Expeditionary Force in France, on behalf of National Air Communications from Exeter Airport.

After thirty-five years concealed in Tiverton golf course shed, a propeller from the Handley Page HP42 crash-landing of 1939 reappears from obscurity in 1975.

In July 1910 the Royal Navy assembled more than 150 warships in Torbay for review by King George V and Queen Mary. Claude Grahame-White is pictured taking off from Abbey Park, Torquay, to fly over the fleet. The centre coach belonged to the Grant Family, of Grant's Marble Works.

A flight of Supermarine Southampton flying boats from 480 Coastal Reconnaissance Flight at Calshot landed in Tor Bay, before returning to Calshot later the same day, 21 September 1926.

G-AFRP, the second Shapley Kittiwake, built by E.S. Shapley at Torquay and first flown at Roborough during 1938.

Hawker Typhoon IB R8635/G of the Royal Aircraft Establishment at Meadfoot Beach, Torquay, after a forced landing, 21 May 1943.